Secrets of A Good Wife

Sex Truths & Other Marriage Essentials

A Christian Woman's Discovery Guide

Mavis McKnight

All scripture quotations in this book were taken from The Bible, New International Readers Version (NIRV) and New King James Version (NKJV)

Copyright © 2018 by Mavis McKnight

ISBN: 978-1-63110-304-9

All rights reserved

Reproduction or transmission by electronic, mechanical, photocopying, recording or otherwise is prohibited without written permission from the author.

Printed in the United States

*To my mother Elvira Queen
who lost her life to breast cancer, but lives on as my source of
strength and wisdom*

*To my Father Bishop Charles C. Queen 1,
who is my champion of faith*

*To all the bold and courageous
wives
willing to bring it to their marriage,
believing in a happily ever after,
striving to be the best wives their husbands could dream of,
and wanting to bring their marriage to a soul-satisfying level*

Contents

Introduction:	**The Good Wife**	**6**

Part One:	**First Things First**	**18**
1.	The Starting Point for Every Good Wife	19
2.	Yes, You Were Chosen to Be Happily Married	25
3.	Self-Knowledge First, All Others Second	31

Part Two:	**Keeping it Real**	**40**
4.	The Marriage Tennis Match – Serve, Receive, Love	41
5.	The Marriage Poison – Unrealistic Expectations	49
6.	The Marriage Killer – Unforgiveness	59
7.	The Marriage Secret Weapon – Prayer	69

Part Three:	**Hubby-ness**	**78**
8.	Hubby, Man, and Leader	79
9.	Hubby and His Homeboys	91
10.	Hubby's #1 Fan and Cheerleader	101
11.	Hubby, Knight, and Superman	113
12.	Hubby's Fun, Sexy, Classy Wife	121

Part Four	**Let's Talk about Sex**	**134**
13.	Your Ultimate Marriage Power Tool – Sex	135
14.	Seven Sexual Power Tools – Plug-In and Practice	145

Part Five:	**Get on your Grind**	**156**
15.	Do the Work	157
16.	Rewards Program	161

Contents

Our Love Story	165
Acknowledgements	169
Source References	172
Recommended Resources	175

Introduction

The Good Wife

"He that finds a good wife better hang on to her for dear life!

~B. Wise

Three strikes and you're out...or is the third time a charm? Suddenly, in the recesses of my mind, an alarm bell went off. A slight tingle of fear moved through my mid-section as I stared at my reflection in the bridal room vanity mirror, on the first day of April, 2006. It was my wedding day—*my third wedding day.*

"What in the world are you doing? You know that almost half of all marriages end up in divorce court, and you have already contributed at least a couple of percentage points to that statistic. What will happen this time?

To my surprise the questions continued like rapid fire. *"What will this marriage be like? How do I know this one will be different? How do I know this marriage won't crash and burst into flames like my first...and my second? What will it really take for me to learn how to be a good wife...this time?"*

For generations, people all over the world have been trying to discover the secrets to a great and lasting marriage. Truth be told, I didn't care enough to wonder about it much in either my first or my second marriage. That quite possibly explains why both crashed and burned.

However, throughout my third, I have come to know that wives hold an enormous share of the power that creates a great marriage. A wife can impact every aspect of her married life. She can build her husband up, and she can tear him down. She can create a happy, harmonious environment, and she can just as easily create a poisonous, undesirable one. She can radiate good energy, and she can spread negative energy. She can make decisions that can and will affect the stability of her marriage.

In a nutshell, her words, actions, behaviors, attitude, and God-given gift of influence have the power to shape the life of her marriage. Just how does that happen?

In the Beginning

In the book of Genesis, Adam and Eve were created. They were perfect, and they communed with God.
They didn't need special rules, procedures, instructions, or policies to maintain a great, loving, sexy marriage. They trusted God—*and each other*—and were content. Adam knew what to do to make Eve happy and fulfilled, and Eve knew what to do to uplift Adam, start his engines roaring, and get him to the train station of pleasure. All was good in the Garden.

Until one day, while Eve was admiring the tree of *knowledge of good and evil*, the serpent slithered up and started a conversation with her.

> *"I see you're admiring that tree."*
> *"Yes, it's peculiar, but beautiful. Why are you in my business?"*
> *"I just thought you might want to pick a piece of fruit and eat it. I'm sure it will taste delectable."*
> *"Oh noooo, God told us not to."*
> *"Oh go on, just one. It won't kill you…The only reason He told you not to eat it is because then you would be a god, powerful and great just like Him."*

Eve's mouth started to water, and her curiosity got the best of her. She picked the fruit, took a bite, and offered a bite to Adam, who stood right next to her. Adam tried to resist, but resistance was futile. His desire was to please Eve. Although God had told Adam not to eat the fruit, Eve's influence, was greater. She eventually persuaded him to violate God's command. This is a screaming example of how her words, actions, and God-given gift of influence, shaped her marriage. Because from that day on she created a life that separated them from God.

God's punishment for Eve was to be in servitude to her husband. And, being that there was no more natural communion with God after that experience, most of Adam and Eve's interactions became strained. Adam was hot and bothered, because Eve had messed up, and Eve was irritated, because she had to serve a man who blamed her for the unhappiness that was now their life.

From that single act of disobedience, the trust was broken, and man and woman ceased to live in natural abundance and peace.

Fast Forward

Sadly, in the world today, one of the only things in abundance is lack. Lack of love. Lack of grace. Lack of communication. Lack of education. Lack of knowledge. Lack of acceptance. Lack of understanding. Lack of wisdom. And lack of desire to learn how to keep a marriage divinely connected and sparkling. As a result, according to Terry Real, a family therapist and founder of Relational Life Institute, 43% of all marriages in America end in divorce. *Tsk, tsk, tsk.*

However, in a society where people have mostly *lost that lovin' feelin'* for marriage, there are a large number of women who haven't strayed and still feel a natural urge to be the very best wives they can be.

You have a choice

Back in the 1940's and 50's, men and women dated, got married, and fulfilled the roles and responsibilities of the husband and wife. The husband went to work all day and brought home the bacon, and the wife stayed home and took care of the house and the children. A *good wife* during those times was expected to cook, clean, wait on her husband hand and foot, and fulfill her husband's sexual needs. Some of you reading this may find that ridiculous and disgusting, but that was the reality of the time.

Today, much has changed. Since the second wave of the Women's Rights Movement and the Sexual

Revolution, married women are much more empowered and self-reliant.

They are no longer in the position where they are forced to *give and serve,* because they are not the bread winners, or looked down upon, because they *bucked the system*. Women are in the position to be able to *choose* whether they *want* to give and serve.

When you have choices, you can and should look to do whatever brings the best possible result for each person involved in the marriage. Translation: The good of the relationship becomes your priority. It supports the success and benefit of the marriage to react calmly and thoughtfully to your husband's requests, even though you may want to raise sand and act ugly.

The definition of a *good wife* has changed. You can still cook, clean, and see to your husband's sexual needs, but now you have the power to choose, and you also have the power to choose to be reciprocated and fulfilled. The key is to use this power in a way that benefits you, your husband, and your marriage.

The heart of her husband doth safely trust in her.

~Proverbs 31:11

The desire of every man is to be able to safely trust his wife with his heart. I am one of those women who strives to fulfill that desire for my husband. I am a woman who is eager to know *how* to be a *good wife* and to apply all that I learn in my pursuit of that knowledge.

Now, I ask you: Are you a wife who is willing to reverse the curse Eve initiated? Are you eager to learn what you can do to make your marriage happier, healthier, sexier, and more fulfilled, engaging, and fun?" If so, you are in luck, because that is my purpose for writing this book.

Your marriage is unique, as is mine. However, there are common factors that affect us all. The information in this book will answer questions you might have about

> *What truly works in marriage?*
> *What do men want from women?*
> *What do men think?*
> *How do men think?*
> *What do men wish women would do?*
> *What do men wish women would not do?*
> *How do I build my sexual self-confidence?*
> *How do I get my sexual needs met?*
> *How do I incorporate this new information into my daily life?*
> *How can I receive the greatest benefit from my work in my marriage?*

Even if you are a woman who thinks you know all there is to know about being a good wife, and you are satisfied with your marriage, I will bet that you can get at least one new idea from this book that can improve and enhance your relationship.

Truth makes all things beautiful.

~Edward Counsel, *Maxims*

If being a good wife with a successful marriage is your desire--*and I would hope that it is, as you've picked up this book*--I have come to tell you about some of the many pathways designed to move you closer to the fulfillment of your desires.

I call these pathways **The Secrets of a Good Wife: Sex Truths, and Other Marriage Essentials:**

1. The Starting Point for Every Good Wife
2. Yes, You Were Chosen to Be Happily Married
3. Self-Knowledge First, All Others Second
4. The Marriage Tennis Match - Serve, Receive, Love
5. The Marriage Poison - Unrealistic Expectations
6. The Marriage Killer - Unforgiveness
7. The Marriage Secret Weapon - Prayer
8. Hubby, Man, Leader
9. Hubby and His Homeboys

10. Hubby's #1 Fan and Cheerleader
11. Hubby, Knight, Superman
12. Hubby's Fun, Sexy, Classy Wife
13. Your Ultimate Marriage Power Tool – Sex
14. Seven Sexual Power Tools – Plug-In and Practice

These Essentials are your tools for enhancing your marriage. What is unique about the information you'll be gifted with is that you will not only learn what these essentials are and how to use them, but you will also be shown birds eye views of the ways in which most wives react in the midst of situations that call for their use. It is my desire to make you aware of your reactions and teach you the *Good Wife's response*, uniquely different from most wives' typical reactions.

I will also share how one of these is "The Mother of Essential Truths Every Good Wife Must Know" *the most powerful tool in the Good Wife's Tool Kit.* I can see you're guessing, aren't you? *It's probably not what you're thinking.*

As you read through this secret toolkit of truths and essentials, it's important that you relax, open your heart, open your mind, and allow this insightful and enriching information to flow into you, and land in your fertile ground of acceptance.

You have a great task before you, and I know you are up for it. These Truths and Essentials--*if practiced*--will help you create and enjoy a more fulfilling, pleasurable, and easy marriage.

A good wife knows to keep a well maintained and diverse array of tools ready at her disposal.

Disclaimer

Before you turn the page, it's important to know that although I am a very candid and straight-forward person, I care deeply about your marriage, your heart, and your well-being. And, be assured that all the information shared here is only intended to help or assist you, never to harm, offend, or embarrass you. My hope is that you receive what I share in that spirit of caring.

Lastly, none of the truths, tips, and nuggets I share are designed to rob you of your personal power. So, be mindful not to over accommodate or become any version of a doormat.

One final note

My goal is to speak to your heart, so that you can speak to the heart of your husband. God has given us all divine gifts, talents, and a purpose. Purpose, changes lives and I intend to use what God has put inside of me, along with my knowledge, research, and personal experiences, to share clearly and candidly what He has for you.

My desire is that it motivates and inspires you to positive action, and that your marriage, your sex life, and your emotional connection will be much stronger and more enriched from it. Now turn the page and begin your journey!

Part One
First Things First

Chapter One

The Starting Point For Every Good Wife

"Above everything else, guard your heart. Everything you do comes from it."

~Proverbs 4:23 (NIRV)

When my hubby and I were first engaged, my fervent prayer to God was to give me everything I would need to help my soon-to-be husband. You see, he was the Pastor of Life Enrichment Ministries in Los Angeles before we met, which meant I would soon step into the role of the First Lady of his church, something I had no clue how to do.

Although my father has been a pastor most of my life, and I saw my mother operate in the 'First Lady' mode, I wasn't really old enough to understand—*nor did I pay much attention to*—what it took to be married to a man in such a prominent and powerful position. However, once my hubby and I were married, I had to learn quickly.

When I asked God to give me what I needed to help my hubby, I had no idea I would need God's help more in my daily married life than in our church life. What I found out—*in a not so pleasant fashion*—was that even though my hubby was a Pastor and an anointed man of God, he was a man first!

Unfortunately, we sometimes learn to put people on pedestals and neglect to see them as regular human beings. And I was oh-so-guilty of that one, which turned out to be a major challenge for me to overcome.

"You don't really know a person until you live with him."
~ Ancient Chinese Adage

Experience has taught me so much truth about the statement, *"You don't really know a person until you live with him."* Our first years together were beautiful and blissful, just as the honeymoon stage is supposed to be. Then it started to get real. Suddenly, the wonderful *'can do no wrong man'* I married began to appear to do a whole lot of things wrong, *like be — a human.* The more comfortable he got with me, the more uncomfortable I got with him. What I mean is this.

All the loving, beautiful thoughts I had in the beginning of our marriage started to disappear, and in came the negative, critical, shaking my head thoughts. Not good. After a while, those negative thoughts started to seep into my heart, and that is when the problems really began.

I'm telling the truth so I can shame the evil one. Truth slices, dices, and heals, then sets you free.

When we first come into this world, our hearts are open, loving and positive, and people can do no wrong. As time goes on, and we start to see things as they really are, our hearts begin to sour. We develop ugly attitudes, and we become critical, bitter, or frustrated, along with a host of other negative emotions and feelings.

But there is one thing about the God we serve that makes me so grateful. When He sees us flying off the path, He will prick us, convict us, or speak directly to us, and let us know it's time to get back on.

Thankfully, that is what He did for me and my marriage. If I had spent any more time in the contrary state I was in, there is no telling what would have happened, or where our marriage might be today. He showed me that I was being too judgmental and that I needed to clean out my heart. I learned that my heart was my life and whatever I put into it would come pour out.

That was the turning point. I decided that I wanted to practice having only good and empowering thoughts about my hubby. The beauty of our God is He reminds us and helps us turn those thoughts around to demonstrate their power in changing our hearts.

Michael Hyatt, a personal development coach, author, and mentor shares three reasons to guard your heart:

Your heart is extremely valuable. It is the essence of who you are. It is your authentic self, the core of your being. It is where all your dreams, desires, and passions live. It is that part of you that connects with God and others.

Your heart is the source of everything you do. If your heart is unhealthy, it has an impact on everything. It threatens your family, friends, ministry, career—and most of all, your marriage. It is imperative that you guard it.

Your heart is under constant attack. We have an enemy who is bent on our destruction. He not only opposes God, but everything aligned with Him. He uses all kinds of weapons to attack our hearts. That is why we have to guard our hearts with all diligence, to protect mentally, physically, and spiritually everything we hold dear.

Psalms 51:10 says, "Create in me a clean heart, Oh God, and renew a right spirit within me." You'll never know the power of this scripture until you practice and let it come alive in you.

A good wife knows that her heart is the most important part of her, and that if she takes care of it, it will take care of her, and in turn will take care of her husband.

One final note

Your heart is the starting point. It holds the key to the way you treat your husband. Embrace the three reasons stated above and—with God—do everything in your power to guard your heart with all diligence. Because everything you do truly does come from it.

Red Carpet Reflections

1. What is the starting point for every good wife?

2. List 3 reasons to guard your heart.

3. What is your main takeaway from this chapter?

Chapter Two

Yes, You Were Chosen To Be Happily Married

"Many are called but few are chosen."

~Matthew 22:14

On a bright, clear, beautiful day, I drove to the parking lot of the park around the corner from my job with the Los Angeles County Probation Department. This was a place of refuge and peace, a place where I could relax, eat my lunch in private, and hear from God. As I sat listening, Walt Larimar, co-author of *His Brain, Her Brain*, was being interviewed on 99.5-KKLA Christian radio. He talked about being asked how he was consistently able to make good decisions. His answer was classic, *"By making so many bad decisions!"*

That is exactly how it was for me in relationships, I thought. I had failed in so many that I had no choice but to learn how *not* to fail. For most of my adult life I didn't know how to be in relationships. Although my parents' marriage looked healthy, I never had an inside view, so I didn't know what 'healthy' required. That ignorance led me into many bad relationships over a period of seven years, followed by two horribly abusive marriages that each lasted over eight years. 24 years of problematic relationships is a lot of years!

One ability God has ripened in me is the ability to problem solve. In 2002, after my second marriage crashed and burned, my quest to find the problem in my relationships led me to *me*. I was the common denominator. It wasn't so much that the "others" needed to change, but it was me. With that realization, I had no choice but to turn the focus inward, and cry out to God, begging Him to help me.

During the next three years, God began to show me my ugly side. He took me into the murky, muddy watered beginnings that clouded my view. He revealed to me my extremely negative, though unconscious, attitude, deep disgust, and disrespect toward men, resulting from suffering sexual violations in my early teens and mistreatment in young adulthood. I cried my guts out. I had some painful truths to face. He led me until I arrived at the mid-way point, where the water was a little clearer.

As I prayed and begged Him to help me change my attitude and mindset about men, He began to cleanse my soul and heal my damaged heart. And as my prayers were answered, I reached the surface, and the water became a breathtakingly beautiful clear blue.

My genius in that process was listening to what God told me and watching what He showed me. Through my willingness, I was able to work through it all with Him and accept the truths about myself. And then I saw the truths about men. That they are Assets. Strong Kings. Valuable. Caring. And, Loving.

As I was in a better place, I asked God to bless me with the type of man who would reflect His idea of marriage. *And that was a game changer*. God sent my adorably wonderful husband to me, and I am truly happy! No more abuse. No more arguing. No more fighting. No more disrespecting. With this gift I received, I made a commitment, like I never had before.

> *I committed to give my marriage to God.*
> *I committed to do whatever it took to keep my marriage together.   I committed to learn to be the very best wife I could be, by making our marriage fun, interesting, exciting, sexy, peaceful, and loving.*

God had chosen me to be a happily married woman when I wasn't looking, and my life has never been the same.

"Many are called, but few are chosen."

~Matthew 22:14

There are many women who are called to be wives. Does the calling require you to automatically accept it? Do you courageously dive in with both feet and go forth to implement the call? Will all your questions about marriage be answered in the beginning or even over time? Will you know exactly what to do and what direction to go?

Not exactly. To be called, *which we all are—in one area or another—*means only that. To be called. To be presented with something. It is up to you to take it on. Or not.

On the other hand, to be *chosen* is altogether different. When you are chosen, there is something set aside specifically for you to do, no matter what you think you *want* to do, or what you think you *should* do. If you're reading this, more than likely you are *already* a wife, engaged, or desire to be a wife; As He did with me, God *chose* you to be a happily married woman, even when you weren't looking. So, whatever your story or your journey looks like, it has led you to this exact place…right where God wants you to be.

A good wife knows that her marriage is a gift few women are honored with, so she honors that gift.

One final note

As I have been invited by God to do something different, and have accepted, I encourage you to do the same. Accept your role, with grace and love, through the heart God has gifted you with, and God will honor you and your marriage. That is a promise.

Red Carpet Reflections

1. How can you learn to make good decisions?

2. List 3 commitments to make for a strong and healthy marriage.

3. What is your greatest takeaway from this chapter?

Chapter Three

~The Mother of All Truths~
Self-Knowledge First, All Others Second

"To know yourself is to love yourself. You will love others more, and be happier in your marriage—and in your life."

~ M. McKnight, M.S.

Essential Truth #1

Before you were the size of a pin head, attached to your mother's womb, God knew you. That is so comforting, isn't it? But do *you* know you? I cannot begin to stress how important it is to know yourself. I remember a time when I had no clue of who I was. I would let other people's opinions and decisions become mine. I would fall right in line with whatever path they were taking, or dictated that I take. I allowed others to lead me around like I was a puppy on a leash, with no direction of my own. Trust and believe me when I tell you that is not a happy place to be. Many women struggle in this area, and if that includes you, I want you to take the information in this chapter very seriously.

You gotta know yourself before you even think of getting to know your hubby, or anyone else for that matter. This truth, in my experience, is the most vital and critical key every good wife should know. That's why I have called it *The Mother of All Truths.* Above all, it is imperative to understand, remember, and cherish this truth. It will help you to become more balanced, confident, whole, and happy in yourself, and as a result, happier and more successful in your marriage. And the bonus is your hubby will appreciate that you care enough about yourself to know and grow.

Farnoosh Brock, author of the *Prolific Living* blog, lists five effective ways you can get to know yourself.

1. Get to know your personality
2. Get to know your body
3. Get to know your core values
4. Get to know your likes and dislikes
5. Get to know your dreams

Genesis 4:1 reads, *"And Adam knew Eve."* This bible verse defines the word "knew" as "having had sexual intercourse; an intimate knowing." Webster's Dictionary defines the word "intimate" as "very private;

closely personal; understanding from close personal connection or familiar experience; inmost, deep within."

What do these definitions say about knowing yourself? That you must go deep. Your effort to get to know yourself cannot be like fuzz sitting on the surface of a peach. Slicing through the skin, all the way to the core, is necessary to get the knowledge that you need, the fruit of who you are, to make decisions that best serve you.

To know yourself is to love yourself. If you learn to accept and value yourself, you will bring more joy into your life and in turn experience more happiness. You will reconnect and bond with your inner *Queen*, the God-part of you; that part that always loves you completely and unconditionally.

If you master this one truth only, you can have it all. Not only will it serve you in your marriage, but also in every area of your life. Please do not—*I repeat, do not*—underestimate the power of self-love and inner connection.

The only requirement is that you redesign yourself from the *inside out*. How do you do that? You must turn the focus on you. Become intimate with yourself first. Get to know you and what pleases you. Affirm yourself. Appreciate yourself. Approve yourself. Respect yourself. Show compassion to yourself. Encourage yourself. Build confidence in YOU. Enjoy YOU. Stop judging yourself. Stop comparing yourself. You must come to a place where you hold yourself in high regard, honor yourself, love being with yourself, and love being YOU.

Imagine yourself as an architect with a contract to redesign a building, to make it new and different. What it means to redesign yourself from the inside out is to renew yourself in a way that is different from how the outside world designed you to be. That is growth. If you are struggling in this area, I can help.

That said, I would be in violation of the laws of ethics if I didn't tell you that, your mission to redesign yourself from the inside out--*should you decide to accept it*—may not be easy. In fact, it won't be. It also may be more difficult for some than for others, and that will depend on how many layers of neglect need to be peeled away.

Additionally, you must forgive yourself for any mistakes you made in the past and understand that mistakes are just experiences that help you discover what you like and don't like, want and don't want, and what you should and shouldn't do. Mistakes are the most effective kind of learning. They guide you back to the strong, able, capable, pure, loving YOU. You must believe that your heart has the answer to most of your obstacles and questions. This is your journey to self-love and self-knowledge, two sides of the same coin.

I'm not a chef, by any stretch of the imagination, but I found the recipe for lasagna to be a great example. As relayed to me by a *Five Star Chef*, she prepares a pan of lasagna by first placing the noodles side by side in the bottom of a baking pan.

She next spreads on a layer of special tomato-basil sauce blend, followed by a layer of turkey meat mixture. Lastly, she adds a layer of cheese mixture. She then repeats this series of steps, continually stacking layer upon layer until the pan is full.

Finally, she adds a layer of her special sauce blend and mozzarella cheese on the top, and places it in the oven. When it's time to serve the lasagna, depending on how many layers it has, she may have to put in extra care and effort to get through all of the layers to the bottom of the pan. But once she tastes her own creation, she knows that the effort to get to the bottom was well worth it.

That is how it is with your *inner Queen*. The bottom layer of lasagna noodles represents your *spirit,* your true self, the self that guides you and loves you with no strings attached. The layers of sauce, meat, and cheeses, are your experiences stacked on top, one after another. Just like the extra effort it takes to get to the bottom of the pan of lasagna, it will take extra effort to reconnect with your true self. But once you taste the flavor of your true self, you will savor it. The joy that comes from discovering the true you, and the elation and fulfillment that come from redesigning yourself from the inside out is *worth more than GOLD!*

Master self-love and see everything in your life change for the better, or get even better than it already is. You'll begin to experience more excitement, delight, connection, contentment, passion, and bliss in your marriage. And if you already are, you'll experience these at an even higher level.

A good wife knows the true meaning of "Know Thyself," and that knowledge of self is the foundation of understanding others and one's interactions with others and the world. She realizes that by knowing herself first, she has experienced the deepest kind of learning, and the result will take her marriage to heights it could never reach before.

One final note

The Mother of all Essential Truths is not about sex, which you may have assumed it would be. *But,* it is directly related to it. Without putting into practice the information in this truth, you will never be completely happy and fulfilled. And with it, you will experience something new and different in your marriage, your sexual union with your husband—*and yourself*, I assure you. But don't just take my word for it. Try it, and watch what happens!

Red Carpet Reflections

1. List 3 ways to get to know yourself.

2. What does it mean to redesign yourself from the inside out?

3. What is your greatest takeaway from this chapter?

Part Two
Keeping It Real

Chapter Four

The Marriage Tennis Match
Serve, Receive, Love

"Just play. Have Fun. Enjoy the game."

~Michael Jordan

Essential Truth #2

Serena Williams is an 11-time Wimbledon and 23 Grand Slam world class tennis champion, and *Sports Illustrated 2015 Sportsperson of the Year*. When she began learning the game, her first assignment was to learn the concept of the game. She then had to learn the fundamentals, which included the terminology, the rules, how to hold the racket, and the level of force needed to hit the ball. Fundamentals are what all of us need to learn about anything we want to be successful at, or master.

Once she grasped the basics, she had to put them into action. Then she had to duplicate those actions again and again. Her practice created perfection, and her perfection created the champion she is today. As I watched her play, I was reminded of how marriage is so much like tennis. A serve in tennis is giving your opponent an opportunity to return the ball, and a serve in a marriage is also *giving,* but to your partner. You receive from your opponent in tennis, and you *receive* from your partner in marriage. In both tennis and marriage, Love is the beginning point. Thus, Serve. Receive. Love. Repeat…Serve. Receive. Love. Repeat…

A good wife knows that marriage is a serve, receive, love process. Even though she may want to stop midway through a serve—be it nurturing or pleasure—because she's tired, irritated, or feels her hubby is acting entitled, she knows that the wiser choice is to practice behaviors that benefit her marriage. And she lives by this code.

My husband shared a story with me from his past about a woman he dated who told him that by age twelve, her mother had trained her to serve her husband. She also told him that if a young lady doesn't know how to serve by the time she's twelve, she will never know how. *Well, I don't agree. I believe anyone can learn to do anything at any age, if they are willing, put their mind to it, and practice it.* My hubby has told me this story again and again, and I finally figured out why.

But first, I had to let him *know* that *I was no one's slave.* Even though I was kind about it, he seemed to have gotten a little offended and started to defend *her* and explain to me—*in no uncertain terms*—that the 'slave concept' is by no means the way he saw it. He told me that the lady's behavior had a lasting impact on him, because he felt respected, honored, and loved. He felt that if more people in relationships were mature enough to serve each other, without keeping score, or feeling something is taken away from them, more couples would end up happier.

My blood boiled a bit, but I am a mature adult, so I shook it off. I realized that the reason he told me that story repeatedly was because there was a message in it for me. My final analysis was that he was right, and instead of being irritated with him for what felt like his comparing her and me by pointing out what I was *not* doing—with all that she *had* done—or exhaust and frustrate myself trying to live up to and compete with *her*, I would simply learn from it and use it as a motivator to strive to serve my hubby a little more each day.

This point takes us back to the Introduction, where I talked about your ability to choose to give and serve and to do what is best for both of you. This is the time when you can take yourself out of the picture and think about the receiver, your hubby. You may be thinking, *"Huh?"* Truth is, you cannot truly give to a person when you're thinking about yourself, keeping score, and thinking—*or saying out loud—"When is it going to be my turn to get served?"*

I know that a lot of times you are tired, annoyed, stressed out and don't want to think about doing anything for your husband. You just want to go to bed! And if he hasn't given to you in a while, that can add more fuel to the fire. However, you know that just as you deserve to receive and be served, so does your husband. So, open your heart, and give to him.

Success in this area does need a certain mindset. Jamila Norman, a female farmer at Patchwork City Farms in Atlanta, Georgia, knows this mindset well. She knows that successfully reaping an abundant harvest requires her to get up early every morning and cultivate her crops. She knows that if she stays in bed, or sleeps late, her crops will suffer, and she may not have a harvest to reap.

This mindset is the same for a good wife. If you don't put in the time and effort to give to your hubby from the heart, a barren love will come back to you. You may wake up one morning and find that all your marriage dreams have perished!

One of the basic elements of tennis is there is someone on the other side to receive your serve, and someone to return the serve to you. This is reciprocity, a requirement for a healthy marriage. It is important that you teach your husband in your gentle, feminine way, to give to you and serve you. How? Embrace your gift of influence—not abuse it or turn it into manipulation. You must also confidently speak up about what you love and appreciate, but with tenderness, softness, and kindness. You know the saying *"You can catch more bees with honey than vinegar?"* That's exactly what I'm talking about.

Let me back up a bit, to clarify what I mean by give and serve. I mean *minister:* to give of yourself for the benefit of another—in this case, your husband. It could be intimate bonding, a love gesture, a back rub or shoulder massage, running his bathwater, bringing him a plate of food when he's tired, listening to him when he shares his heart, comforting him, giving him private pleasure (whatever that may mean to you), or any number of things. It is simply you *choosing* to give and serve him from your heart.

Unfortunately, there is a poison that breaks the cycle of reciprocity. That poison is selfishness. Webster's Dictionary defines selfish as, *"being concerned primarily with one's own interests, benefits, welfare, etc., regardless of others."*

I facilitate a monthly Women's Enrichment Study where we tackle topics ranging from beauty, body image, menopause, forgiveness, and celibacy, to pornography, friendship, shopping, addiction, and sex—*just to name a few*. The topic of a recent meeting asked the women, *"Are you marriage material?"* I cited Brooke Dean's article, *Are You Marriage Material? 8 Signs You May Not Make a Good Wife*. Topping the list of signs was Selfishness and explained all sorts of negative behaviors associated with selfishness. These included: not reciprocating; not being good at compromise; not sharing him with family and friends; and holding your partner responsible for your happiness.

Dean's final recommendation to women was to give marriage a second thought. What she meant was, *don't get married if these describe you*. Strong words, but powerful advice. Marriage is a serve, receive, love process. You serving and him receiving, plus him serving and you receiving equals love. If the focus of the one serving is on the receiver, selfishness is eliminated from the equation, and no one feels the need to keep score.

LOVE is the starting score for both tennis and marriage. When a couple marries, all separateness from their past is put behind them, and they start fresh, at ground zero. From this foundation, they can both begin to learn the meaning of loving one another in a new way. Most couples are in love before they unite. But matrimonial love is a different kind of love. Marriage love—*like serving—is a choice and an action*.

"And now these three remain: faith, hope and love. But the greatest of these is love."

~1 Corinthians 13:4-8

A good wife knows that her marriage is like a tennis match—serve, receive, and love—and that of the three, love takes the most practice to perfect her game.

One final note

Although there will be plenty of ups and downs in your marriage journey, it would do a couple well to commit to try to out-love each other. There will be times when choosing to love will be easy, *and there will be times when all you want to do is whack a club upside your husband's head.* Those are the times when the act of love must step in. My hubby shares with me all the time that, in order for him to keep demonstrating his love for me, he has to forgive any and all of my transgressions immediately, and follow up with an act of love. I find that so amazing! But that is exactly what you must do if you are to stay in a good and godly place of continual blessings in your marriage.

Red Carpet Reflections

1. Describe how marriage is like a tennis match.

2. Explain how a female farmer's mindset can relate to your marriage.

3. What is your greatest takeaway from this chapter?

Chapter Five

The Marriage Poison
Unrealistic Expectations

*"There is a way which seems right to a woman in her marriage,
But its end is the way of destruction."*
~Proverbs 14:12

Essential Truth #3

WARNING: POISON KILLS! If you look under your kitchen or bathroom sink right now at the labels of some of your house cleaning items, you will see a warning, "Poisonous If Swallowed" and instructions on how to flush out the toxic chemicals and avoid a fatal disaster.

The instructions in this chapter will help you avoid the danger of a fatal marriage disaster: Managing unrealistic expectations.

First, let's talk about *reality*. At times I have lived outside of *reality*, and other times inside of it. One thing I can thankfully say is that I prefer living inside of it...*most of the time*. Sometimes it can be refreshing to live outside of it, as long as no one gets hurt—including you. Daydreaming, for example, may help you to escape something that may be too hard to deal with at the time—which is not a bad thing, if it calms or relaxes you, or relieves your stress. *But please draw the line there.*

Depending where your daydreams take you, you may find yourself drowning in unrealistic expectations—a surefire path to the destruction of your marriage.

A good wife knows that living outside of reality, with unrealistic expectations, can poison her marriage. Even though she might harbor thoughts like, '*Why is he always at work when he's supposed to be home with me; Or, he needs to take me out to dinner or for a night on the town; Or, he's not the man I thought he was going to be; Or, I didn't sign up for this,*' she knows to relax, curb her demands, and find a new perspective. She also knows that everything is not going to happen the way she *expects* it to all the time. She is more realistic than that.

What exactly does unrealistic mean? In a nutshell, *fantasy*. According to Dictionaryreference.com, fantasy is defined as *"a hallucination, illusion, far-fetched notion, imagination unrestricted by reality; a series of pleasing mental images, usually serving to fulfill a need not gratified in reality."*

Ok, now what is an expectation? An expectation is *"to look forward to; regard as likely to happen."*

Sometimes, fantasy and expectations can work wonders, like when you're working on the manifestation of your dreams and desires. But when you project your fantasy or expectations onto another person, *expect* a major disappointment.

There was a young lady engaged to a man who earned minimum wage. She was unemployed at the time, and had three young children. Even though she was well aware of his income upon entering the marriage, she began announcing to everyone that she was expecting him to buy her a house, a car, jewelry, take her on expensive vacations, and other things. She started to pressure him about it all.

After they married, they had two more children. Her husband never progressed, was never promoted, and never received an increase in his wages. He began to grow more and more disheartened, mainly because—*as a man*—he would have loved to be able to provide things for his wife and children, but he wasn't in a position to do so.

His wife became angrier and more frustrated, adding to the pressure she had already heaped onto him, until one day he cracked. In an unexpected burst of anger, he declared his intention to file for divorce. And, unfortunately, she ended up back where she started, a single mother, but with five mouths to feed, rather than three.

This is absolutely, *not* what you want to happen. Don't get me wrong; you need to have expectations and standards. Without them, you'll be tossed like a ship in a storm without a sail. But you must maintain some sense of reality. You must get to know the difference in the ways that men and women think.

What *you* may consider important, your man might not really care that much about, and vise versa. Her's a perfect example: You may want your man to put the toilet seat down, but he may not see anything wrong with leaving it up; in his mind, you can lift it up for him just as easily as he can put it down for you! A good wife knows to just grin and bear it—*until she can get her own bathroom and put a "No Males Allowed" sign on the door!* Just kidding... *not! This is my reality.*

Unrealistic expectations can cause you to pile on judgment. When you're stuck in a judgmental mindset, you might get mean and tight-jawed every time things don't go your way. Spiritual teacher, Marianne Williamson, talks about *"Creating space for love."* I tweaked her phrase a bit to say, *Creating space for understanding.*

Understanding eliminates judgment. If the wife has a better understanding of who her husband really is, she is less likely to become frustrated with him or the situation. Judging is not cute. I should know; I have had an ongoing dialog with God about helping me to release the judgments I have. *Hey, I'm still a work in progress.*

If you're like most women—*me included*—you might find this one a bit challenging. Just continue to work on relaxing and letting go of the judgment and unrealistic expectations. And, I don't mean to relax your work in areas that help you to grow, or that you should sacrifice anything valuable to your inner growth and self-love. When you're busy doing things you love, like painting, reading, cooking, gardening, skiing, motorbiking, dancing, listening to music, getting a massage, etc., while your hubby is at work or involved in his own pleasures, those are *your* times. You don't *need* him to spend time with you during *your* times.

On the other hand, sitting at home every night, bored and alone, while your hubby is at work, can wear on your nerves. Nights like these can become a constant reminder that you don't spend enough time together, eating away at you as you think about what your hubby *should* be doing. It can cause you to be frustrated and angry—maybe even bitter toward him—resulting in your taking an immature, whiney stance and start to demand time from him that he just doesn't have.

And then if he doesn't respond the way you want him to, you may start to heap guilt trips on him. These are your growth moments; Moments where you reflect, take time to see where you can improve who you are, and moments to find things that interest you as an individual and get involved there. And, most of all moments to remember that from his point of view, he is working hard to take care of you and your family.

Let me share this. One of the most important factors for a man is when and how he earns his money. So, you most likely will have to play second fiddle to that priority, *but an important and valuable second fiddle!* You just need to put on your big girl panties, be a grown up, recognize it for its truth, and give up the jealous pout. Ask yourself: *Am I being fair? Do I need an attitude adjustment?*

After all, you are the main beneficiary of his hard work. You need to pick and choose your battles. Some things you can work on with your husband and some things you will have to accept. Remember, women pay way more attention to the details in a relationship than men do. *Hey, I know, somebody has to do it. Just be realistic about it.*

A good wife knows to expect no more than a man shows her in the beginning of their relationship, and that if she accepts and shows appreciation for all that

he is, without wanting anything that he is not, he will likely surprise her with more than she could have imagined.

One final note

You can rest assured that when you master this Essential Truth, it will benefit you and work in your favor in ways you might never envision. Your hubby may respond in such positive ways, he may just blow your mind. It will certainly take pressure off him and that is a plus in any husband's book!

Red Carpet Reflections

1. List 1-2 ways unrealistic expectations can poison your marriage.

2. In what context does fantasy and expectations work wonders?

3. What is your greatest takeaway from this chapter?

Chapter Six

The Marriage Killer Unforgiveness

"If you don't forgive others their trespasses, God will not forgive yours."

~ Matthew 6:15

Essential Truth #4

I find it so fitting to start this chapter with the above scripture, to help you see the danger and seriousness of unforgiveness. I don't know about you, but those words are pretty scary to me. I know I need forgiveness every single day. So, I strive hard to work on forgiving others.

Forgiveness is such an issue for many a wife. Emotional hurts, pains, and disappointments sometimes seize something deep inside and won't seem to let go. But a good wife knows that everyone has caused someone pain, everyone has made mistakes, and everyone needs forgiveness. *Even though she might want to harden her heart, roll her eyes, and smirk at her husband,* a good wife knows that holding on to something only works when she is waiting for something good or miraculous to happen. *When she is in a dark place of unforgiveness, she continues to damage her soul.*

What is forgiveness, and why is it so hard to offer? Is forgiveness a dirty word? Let's put some bleach on it, clean it up a bit, and look at it for what it really is. Forgiveness is releasing the need to seek revenge for being wronged in some way that caused you deep pain, sadness, or discomfort. Is it the pain that makes forgiveness so difficult? Or, is it the comfort you feel as you wallow in your hurt? Or, is it that you don't want to let the person(s) off the hook, because they might hurt you again?

When you think about it, forgiveness is big. It reaches to the highest mountain and flows to the lowest valley. Oh, those are the lyrics to *"The blood that Jesus shed for me."* Ok, nothing actually compares to what Christ did for us by giving His life, but forgiveness is definitely on the list of big things.

Speaking of lists, might there be someone other than your husband whom you've had the darndest time forgiving? Maybe your parents? *Check.* Your siblings? *Check.* Your children? No check for me, thank God, but maybe for you? Your boss or co-workers? *Check.* Your friend, past lover, or ex? *Check. Check. Check.*

Did your hands involuntarily go to your hips in a defiant stance of unforgiveness? I mention the other possible recipients of your unforgiveness only for your benefit, because once you learn how to forgive, you can see all the places and persons you've held back from, and aim to offer it to each of them.

Connie Domino, Master of Public Health and Registered Nurse, wrote a book called *The Law of Forgiveness.*

Now you may be thinking, *What? Law? Oh goodness, does that mean I have to obey it?* Well…*why not?*

Obeying this law would have worked well for a couple I knew. They had been married for over twenty years. The husband became addicted to drugs and lost everything, their home, cars, jewelry, his job, *and his dignity*. Even though his wife was devastated by his choices and his behavior, she made the decision to stay with him and weather that storm. However, she never truly forgave him. Now they live together in misery.

Of all people, I know that forgiveness is not always easy, and we all have our deal breakers. But if you are committed to your marriage, and you choose to stay after a major violation or betrayal, *you must be committed to forgiveness.* You need to release your husband—*and yourself*—from the destructive bondage of unforgiveness.

Beware of grudges, the poison daggers that can—and will—kill. Grudges cause wreckage and ruin the happiness and sanctity of your marriage, and your life.

"And for love's sake, each mistake you forgave."

~ Nick Ashford and Valerie Simpson

Husband and wife writing production team and Songwriter's Hall of Fame inductees, Nick Ashford and Valerie Simpson were married for more than thirty-five years. In their song *Solid,* they wrote about forgiving for the sake of love, getting serious and sticking it out, staying the course, and building trust.

And as a result, they learned to love deeper and create a rock solid marriage foundation. Do you think they came up with those lyrics off the top of their heads? No, *they lived them!*

Is there something you are holding against your husband, something that you just cannot seem to get over for the life of you? If you hold on to grudges, it will do you well to step back and look at your husband through his eyes, and through his soul. See the child inside, the tender heart, the one who has been through countless childhood hurts and pains, the one who loves you and wants only to be loved by you. When you can do this, it becomes easier to forgive, deepen and strengthen your love, and build a solid foundation for your marriage to grow and last.

If not, you may be doomed to a life of misery. And why be together, if you're not really *together*?

What if you don't *want* to forgive, or *think you can't forgive?* Connie Domino says that the negative consequences of holding onto unforgiveness can cause depression, anger, negative thoughts and feelings, low self-esteem, and can even show in your slumping posture. It can hold you to the past and prevent you from being able to move forward. It can create weight gain, exhaustion, physical disabilities, illness, and physical ailments. Holding onto unforgiveness can choke the life out of you and your marriage. It can—*and will*—affect every area of your life, from your work, to your health, to your finances.

Wow! You can clearly see why God wants you to forgive. His thoughts of your happiness don't include any of those awful things. His thoughts are only to prosper you and give you a good future and good fortune (*Jeremiah 29:11*).

Of course, there are things that will be more challenging to forgive, but that is where you can put your trust in God. Someone in my past poured so much dirt on me that I had to reach deep to release the bitterness and anger I harbored. Although you too may have to reach deep, forgiveness releases the hold on you, your marriage and your life.

> *"Forgiveness causes things to move fast, so buckle your seatbelt."*
> *~Katherine C. Giovanni*

When you start forgiving, be prepared for things to start moving and changing—*for the better*! You're probably itching to know what you can do and what steps you can take, to be able to forgive. The steps below are ones I used from *The Law of Forgiveness,* and they work well for any person, or situation that needs forgiveness, *including yourself.*

Steps to Forgiveness

1. Develop a goal-related affirmation for your marriage. For example, "*My relationship with my husband now has more love, care, acceptance, patience, and understanding.*"

2. State the forgiveness affirmation. For example, "*I forgive you completely and freely. So far as I am concerned the incident(s) that happened between us is finished forever. I hold you in the light, and all is well between us.*"
3. Have a soul-to-soul visual conversation with your husband. This begins with visualization. Bring your husband into your mind's eye and be sure he is in a happy state. State the problem, the emotion, the solution, and the consequences. Repeat your forgiveness affirmation. Then forgive it all.

Sometimes forgiveness is quick, as it was when I forgave my brother for the atrocity, he committed against me and my family. Sometimes it takes a while, as it did when I forgave my son's father for all of the humiliation, hurt, and despair he caused. Either way, it's all good for your soul.

If you want to be happy, forgive. Forgiveness—*like healing*—comes from God. It is supernatural. Give it, and bask in it.

The next time you're confronted with an issue of unforgiveness, use these amazing tools. However you get there, whether through prayer, forgiveness exercises, or your relentless pursuit of it, forgiveness will transform you and your marriage.

Forgiveness is not an option it is a command!

Since we are exploring forgiveness, *we need to look at sincerity.* Sincerity means to be genuine and real. As hard as it may be, you must work to be sincere about forgiving. If you are not sincere, don't expect anything positive to happen, or any mountains to move…not even a pebble. Sincerity is the key.

Can you think of someone who was able to forgive someone of a cruelty inflicted upon them? Straight off the bat, I think of Jesus Christ. *Uh huh, you didn't think I was going to go there, did you?*

There are others, I'm sure, who come to your mind. Just know it is possible to sincerely forgive. If others can do it, so can you. *Don't you hate when people say that? I do too sometimes, but it's the truth.*

To be able to forgive sincerely, you need to use a little thing call grace. Without grace, there is no forgiveness. They go hand in hand. According to the bible, grace is *"unmerited favor; your receiving something you did nothing to deserve."* Some people are so much better at offering grace than others. Case in point, my hubby versus me.

A couple years ago I asked my hubby to go into the garage and find the box that contained our taxes from the previous year. He searched for four days, pulling out every box and looking in each one, trying diligently to find the taxes. On the fourth day he said, *"That box is not in the garage."* Of course, I made a face that he later told me said, *"Men can't do anything; I'm just going to have to find it myself!"*

So, I began pulling boxes down asking, *"Did you check these?"* saying, *"The box has to be here,"* with all my exaggerated gestures and antics. After a few failed attempts, I went back into the house and looked inside one particular box that had been in the house for about two months, convinced that I had thoroughly searched it already. I lifted two or three items in the box, and what did I find? The taxes! Right away, I went outside and said, *"Sweetie..."* He knew immediately, by the tone of my voice, that I had found the taxes. I apologized profusely. I felt so bad. What do you think he said? *"Don't worry about it; forget it; it's alright. I'm just glad you found them."* WHAT? I was dumbfounded. I could not believe the grace he showed me. I did not feel I deserved it, or earned it; in fact, I felt I deserved the opposite.

What I realized in that experience is that it takes a lot of care, concern, patience, and love, to be able to offer grace. And, to give both sincere forgiveness and grace, we need to access the love inside of us, that God love. We all have the ability, but too often, negativity builds a covering around our hearts, and it seems love is not there. But it is always there. We just need to bring it out from behind the covering and place it into the forefront. This takes effort and practice, but it can be done. Focus on the person who will benefit from your love, forgiveness, and grace.

A good wife knows that with God's help, she can forgive what she thinks she can't.

One final note

Forgiveness feeds love, respect, peace, integrity, and kindness. When you forgive, you notice your head becomes less foggy, your energy shifts, your heart opens, and all is great with the world. Imagine a marriage that has these benefits, all from you deciding to forgive your husband! You may even be able to write your own book on Joy and Happiness 101. Are you game?

Red Carpet Reflections

1. Define forgiveness.

2. List 3 benefits of forgiveness.

3. What is your greatest takeaway from this chapter?

Chapter Seven

The Marriage Secret Weapon
Prayer

"Call to me and I will answer you and tell you great and unsearchable things."

~Jeremiah 33:3

Essential Truth #5

Many times, we think that most of our issues have solutions with practical steps to follow, which is true. However, some answers can only come from God through prayer. And I'm not talking about *"Our Father who art in Heaven hallowed be Thy name, Thy Kingdom come, Thy will be done on earth as it is in Heaven."* That surely has its time and place, but not here. We need to go deeper.

A good wife recognizes that prayer is her secret weapon. She sincerely prays for her husband and asks God to give her what she needs to be his helpmate and the best wife she can be. Even though she might want to say, *"I want to be a good wife and everything, but do I really have to pray?"* she knows the answer is yes. She knows that prayer is non-negotiable and should be the foundation of her marriage.

I have heard the story many times over about how women have dreamt of their wedding day since they were young girls. You may have been one of them. If you were, you probably thought about your dress, the venue, the decorations, walking down the aisle to your prince charming, and every small detail. Your heart and mind were open and sincere, and you felt deeply and believed in all that you wanted. You connected with something inside of you, even if you weren't aware of what that something was.

This is the same place you connect with when you sincerely pray for your husband. You open up your heart and mind all the way and connect with God in full belief and anticipation. You say the words with feeling and emotion and really mean what you are asking for. You believe that God will answer every question, concern, or petition about your husband, your marriage, and yourself that you put before Him. And after you do, you can expect answers. He will give them to you. Remember, this *is God* we're talking about.

Now I know this is all good and perfect when all is great with you and the world, but what if your husband just did something that hurt your feelings, or touched that last nerve? What if you don't even like him right now? Ephesians 4:26 tells us, *"Don't let the sun go down on your wrath."* But what if you're angry at your husband and you did *"let the sun go down on your wrath?"* Then you woke up the next morning not wanting to say your prayers, because you knew they included prayers for your hubby and you weren't feeling all that great about him. But you said them, only because you knew you were supposed to…

I remember being in a similar situation. The morning after, I got down on my knees to say my prayers, but my head and my heart were nowhere near the right place. I tried to focus my spirit and mind for a few minutes, but nothing happened, except more of the negative talk inside me. I said, *"You know what God? I can't even get it together right now. My mind is all over the place and I have a serious attitude, so I'm not even going to play like I can do this. I'm not even going to waste Your time, or mine."* But then I just continued anyway and recited my usual prayers, *Thank you for this, that, and the other*, completely from my head, conveniently leaving out any reference to my hubby, and said amen and got up. Was there anything sincere about that latter prayer? NO!

As you read that scene, did you think there would be a happily ever after ending, that I'd be able to bring all my goodness and godliness to bear and conquer my challenge? Well, *it didn't happen.* What did happen was that I realized I could not go into a prayer for my husband with my heart full of stuff like, *He gets on my nerves; he makes me sick; what was I thinking when I married this dude,* and any other thoughts of like passion. And neither can you.

Instead, you must, *and I repeat—YOU MUST*—first bow down and surrender that negative spirit to God and ask Him to cleanse your heart, to get all the garbage out so He can get into it. God gets into it when you get yourself *–and your ego*—out of it. Then you ask God for forgiveness. First John 1:9 says that if you ask God for forgiveness, He is just and willing to forgive you. That is how your heart gets cleaned out and how you get into alignment with God. Then—*and only then*—will your prayers be sincere enough to be heard by God. The cherry on top is your absolute belief that God can and will answer your prayers.

Well, that's actually the ice cream. The cherry is his answering. Hopefully, you get my drift.

If you're still having difficulty bringing your mind to a place of fertile ground for sincere prayer, there is one more thing that will benefit your husband, your marriage, and yourself. Stormie Omarian, author of *A Praying Woman,* says that to bring your mind into a positive place, practice thinking daily on Philippians 4:8. This scripture says to think on things that are true, things that are noble, things that are just, things that are pure, things that are lovely, things of a good report, things of virtue, and things of praise.

She tells us that if we think on these things, we won't be stuck focusing on anything critical that keeps us in a bad frame of mind. These are wise words. I must admit, it has worked wonders for me. These are God's instructions to you as a believer. And you know you need to do what God tells you, right? You do, if you want to have the kind of marriage that takes you to the highest Himalayas and represents and glorifies God!

One final point. I've had a lot of training in many different job fields over the years. One of my jobs was a security guard. My former husband was deeply interested in law enforcement and dreamed of becoming a police officer. He thought it would be a great idea if we both trained in the field and, though reluctant, I agreed. One aspect of our training was role play.

Here was the scene. One person acted as a criminal and tried to take the officer's weapon away, while the other person acted as the police officer with the weapon. When it was my turn as police officer, I struggled against my *criminal's* desperate attempts to take my weapon. He was much bigger and stronger than I, but I was determined to wrestle him and overcome those obstacles to win. We spun around in circles endlessly, until he was finally able to reach my gun and take it away from me. I had lost, and that felt horrible.

This scene is a lot like the way many husbands and wives function in their marriage. They try to fight *the bigger enemy of their marriage* all by themselves, and they end up losing the battle. This is why it is so important to have God in the center of your marriage and, through sincere prayer, continually place your hubby and yourself with God. Your prayers can be requests for more patience, more love and understanding, insight and wisdom, more respect, good health, a sound mind, more chemistry, more openness, more intimacy, more trust, (add your own). Just ask God and believe. He will give you what you need.

A good wife knows that prayer is her secret weapon—a foundational weapon—that guards and keeps her marriage safe from both inner and outer attacks.

One final note

I want to reiterate that sincere prayer is not about just saying the words out of your head and expecting your prayers to be answered. When you pray for your husband and your marriage, take the above guidance to heart and align with God. Prayer done the right way is forgiveness, intercession, and fellowship with God. Then, as Jeremiah 33:3 says, listen for God to give you a prophetic word. Lastly, speak it and live it! With prayer as your secret weapon—it is one secret that you can share with the world!

Red Carpet Reflections

1. Why is it important that prayer be the foundation of your marriage?

2. List 3 prayer request you can petition to God for your husband.

3. What is your greatest takeaway from this chapter?

Part Three
Hubby-ness

Chapter Eight

Hubby, Man, Leader

"Your marriage is not a competition. It is part of your life's work."

~ Deborah Mills, BMWK

Essential Truth #6

My father always uses the phrase, "It's a sad commentary" when he refers to something that strikes him as a sin and a shame. It's my turn to use that phrase.

It's a sad commentary when a wife finds it necessary to compete with her husband for the lead role, instead of doing her best as a supporting actress.

One thing I've noticed again and again is that a lot of women find it a challenge to respect their husband's role as 'the Man' in the marriage. A major factor in your husband's ability to gain confidence in who he is as a man, is your allowing him to take the lead. A good wife knows how to let her hubby be the man, make some decisions, and have the last word—even though she might think, *He doesn't have the sense he was born with* (oooh, did I write that?)! And, although she might want to argue him into the ground, because she just *knows* she is smarter than he is, she also knows to let him be the man, let him make some decisions, and let him have the last word…*sometimes*.

I have to ask you, *What is the problem with letting your husband be 'the Man' and take the lead and have the leadership role in your marriage?* Let's take a peek at something. Have you ever asked your hubby to fix something, or put something together, and he just took *forever* to do it? And you got impatient and started fixing and putting things together on your own, because *he's never going to get it done, or do it right anyway*? The answer is probably a resounding YES! Did you stop to think what that may have done to his manhood, his self-esteem? That likely crushed it. *And I'm exaggerating only a tiny bit.*

I remember a comedian once said that whenever his wife would ask him to do things he didn't want to do, he would do them wrong on purpose, because he knew she would storm in and take over the job. Then he'd be off the hook. Now that may have been funny as a joke, but in real life, one of the most powerful truths is:

> *Men need us to need them.*

Did you know that one of the top needs of a man is to be needed? According to an article I read recently, many men wonder what the point is in being married to, or in relationship with, a woman who doesn't need him. *Let that one sink in for a minute.*

I remember about four years into our marriage when my hubby told me that I was a married woman acting like I was still single. *Ouch.* I didn't want to hear that one, but it was the truth. In other words, I was still doing many of the things he could do for me.

Why do we women sometimes have such a take-over spirit? In their best-selling book, *His Brain, Her Brain*, authors Walt and Barb Larimore talk about the differences in the design of the male and female brains and how the differences affect everything we do. Their research shows that both male and female embryos begin with female brains. These female brains contain millions of communication connectors between the right and left brain hemispheres, so that both sides of the brain can communicate with each other, enabling us to simultaneously process emotions, feelings, thoughts, and solutions.

Then, during the first six weeks of development, male embryos go through a stage in which is called a *testosterone bath.* During this stage, they develop male sex hormones and other male traits. What also occurs during this stage is the majority of their brain communication connectors are severed. Once the severing is complete, the male communication functions slow considerably, and their ability to simultaneously process emotions and solutions disappears. *Wow!*

Because our female brain connectors stay intact, we continue to process thoughts, feelings, emotions, and solutions simultaneously, and at a much quicker rate—in fact double that of men. *That's where the impatience comes in. I bet you didn't realize that, huh?* Since most of us aren't knowledgeable of this, nor are we conscious of it in the moment, we see men's *inability to do what we do* as their being lazy, slothful, slow, or inattentive. And because most women have control issues—*yes!*—stemming from our nurturing, caring, maternal urges and instincts, —*and our belief that we know everything*—we think our speed, ability, and methods make us better and right.

When we step in and *take over,* our men end up scratching their heads, feeling unappreciated, irritated, frustrated, and disrespected, because we've robbed them of the opportunity to feel useful and needed. *We have stolen their opportunity to be men.*

While we're on the subject of your husband being the man, an area most women lack self-control in, is decision-making. You're probably thinking, *Hey I didn't buy this book to be talked down about.* And that is certainly not my intention. My intention is only to help, not to hurt. And if you are sincerely seeking the truth, be a woman *of* truth, and let the truth set you free. The truth is: Every man wants to feel like he is able to make competent, *translation, 'successful'* decisions for his marriage, family, career, and life in general. When God designed the man, He designed him to be a protector, a provider, a priest, and a leader. This design has a direct effect on the way he sees everything. And with these goals innately functioning, he views his results as either Success or Failure.

Alright, I know you are smart. I know you are intelligent. I know you can run circles around your man's head *(oooh, did I write that?)*. I know you have influence. I know you can use your womanly wiles and come up with devious schemes and plans to get what you want—*maybe not devious— but plans all the same.* And I know that you may be able to make better decisions in certain situations. But, in all truthfulness: *you don't know everything.* Even though you know a lot, you don't know everything. There are some things only your man has the answers to and is able to make decisions about. This division of abilities is called Balance. God did that. So, take your complaints up with Him—if you dare.

Because you don't know everything, you cannot make wise or correct decisions about everything. Part of your responsibility as a wife is to help your husband grow and become a proficient and evolved man and leader. You must give him a chance to make decisions and make mistakes. Mistakes are how we learn and grow. If you don't give him a chance to make mistakes and learn better from them, he will never become the strong leader God created him to be, and the man you will be proud of.

To gain more clarity, look at it this way. You are a coach of a basketball team with a young new point guard. *Basketball is my favorite sport, so bear with me.* If you never allow your new point guard to take risks and chances in his decisions about what kind of pass to make, or who to pass the ball to, in order to ensure a score, he'll never realize his potential, develop his confidence, or be able to use the experience to learn and grow and become a proficient player.

I'm not saying you shouldn't watch the situation from the sidelines. Yes, do that, because you are a team. Just pray that if he needs assistance he will come to you, but if he doesn't, continue to support and encourage him in this area. Let him drive the car; just be a passenger sometimes instead of the complaining back seat driver. *Even if the engine is smoking, the breaks are squeaking, and the tires are losing air! Well, not really, but you get my drift.*

Speaking of driving, I have to share this little story. My hubby is such a passenger seat driver, always telling me what to do, how to drive, and saying things in a panic like *"You see that car?"* and of course it's a big challenge to hold my tongue while I want to scream, *"Yeah I see that car. I've only been driving for over forty years!"* Anyway, I came across some information on why men do that. *They actually believe they're going to die when we're behind the wheel! Wow!* Now I know what I'm dealing with—and hopefully you will too if you find yourself in a similar situation.

Please believe that at some point you will get an opportunity to put your two cents in during certain situations. Until then, mind your own business. I know, *he is your business*, but you know what I mean. And, when that time does come, be gentle. If he fails, he is already in the dumps about it. Don't make it worse. That is not your job. Your job is to make it better. So, whether your man is an alpha male, a beta male, or an omega male, he needs to work and earn money, be free to make decisions, be supported and encouraged, be affirmed and appreciated, and feel needed and successful. The more successful he is, the more he will want to do. *Remember, you're the lucky recipient of his work.* Help him to step up as a leader for your marriage and family, his rightful place.

Learn how your hubby defines himself as a man. In many of my talks with couples about marriage and relationships, there is one statement from women I hear too often, "*You ain't no man.*" Imagine what this does to a man's very soul. I'll give you an example. The movie *Money Monster* focused on a so-called 'financial wizard' who gave stock investment advice in a weekly television show. To boost ratings, the *Money Monster*—George Clooney—began his show by rating the hottest stocks to attract investors. But little did the viewers' know, the stock ratings were bogus. They followed his advice to the letter.

In a dramatic turn of events, one stock option that he had rated *Hot* plummeted, draining the accounts of most of its investors, one of whom lost every penny he had saved for his fiancée and their unborn child. Determined to get an explanation for the stock's overnight fall and hold the *Money Monster* accountable, the now broke investor came to the station with guns and dynamite a blazing, and took the *Money Monster—and anyone close to him*—hostage.

When the station manager and security discovered the investor's identity, they contacted his fiancée, hoping that she could talk him down. But, instead of coaxing him with kind and nurturing words, she began cursing him and calling him everything but a child of God. The most devastating part of her rant was when she screamed,

"You call yourself a man? You ain't no man; you're an idiot, a fool!" Hearing her words sucked the life right out of the now devastated man; took the wind out of his sails, rendering him worthless.

I want to suggest that you be very careful when you are about to criticize your man. A good wife takes time to get to know her man's worth. His manhood is directly tied to his worth and value, just as your womanhood is directly tied to yours. Try as hard as you can to keep the *"You ain't no man"* declaration out of your heart—and out of your mouth. He may only be doing what he thinks is best for the situation at hand. Learn his self-definition of a man, and whatever those traits are, allow him to demonstrate them to you.

> *A good wife knows the ease of marriage that comes when she embraces and expresses her natural feminine abilities and allows her husband to know and express his natural masculine abilities, and that the greatest joy and passion result when there is no competition, only appreciation.*

One final note

Yes, you may have your own opinion of what a man is, but remember, women think completely differently from men. What your definition of a man is may have no resemblance to the way your man defines himself. You would do well to first learn what defines you as a woman. Then when you master being that—in all your feminine, sexy, soft, and gentle beauty—your man will open up and be 'the Man' you so desire and deserve. *Now doesn't that feel better?*

Red Carpet Reflections

1. What is one of the top needs of a man?

2. God designed your husband to be a 1) _____ 2) _____ 3) _____ 4) _____ .

3. What is your greatest takeaway from this chapter?

Chapter Nine

Hubby and His Homeboys

*'Women give men a special type of comfort, but a guy's friends are just different.
Many guys find relaxation or peace when they hang out with the fellas."*
~Aja

Essential Truth #7

In director Malcolm D. Lee's romantic comedy, *The Best Man*, there was a scene where a group of old friends came to town for a wedding. The fellas decide to hang out. But the girlfriend of one of the fellas interrupted their discussion, to insist that her man come with her and work on their relationship issues—and that it needed to be done *that night*. He gently reminded her that their outing had already been planned. She put on her pouty lip sad face and said, *"Well go on and hang out with them then, since they're so much more important to you."* As you can probably guess, her deliberately manipulative guilt trip made him cave, and she got her way.

Although this is a common scene in many marriages, a good wife knows to encourage her husband to spend time doing things he enjoys, whether alone or with his friends. Even though she might want to play *Eye Spy Private Eye,* look through his cell phone calls and text messages for anything to "catch him on", try to guilt him into staying home with her, or don an attitude from here to eternity, a good wife knows it's healthy and beneficial for him to spend time hanging out with himself and his homeboys, because it is good for his soul.

This is an important truth to explore, because it's not happening as often as it should. Why not? Let's look a little deeper at what the real problem may be. Why do some women take issue with their men spending time away from them? *Is it jealousy? Insecurity? Immaturity? Let's examine.*

Jealousy. What is it? What causes it? What happens when jealously enters the picture? Here is a short lesson in 'Jealousy 101.' Hara Estroff Marano, one of *Psychology Today* magazine's senior contributors, says that even though jealousy is somewhat hard to put an exact finger on, it involves feelings of distress, like fear, abandonment, loss, sorrow, anger, betrayal, envy, and humiliation. *Dang!*

Hara also reveals that something else may be at the center of women's jealousy of not having their husband's full and constant attention. Attachment experiences—*you know*—how safe and attended to you felt with your parents or guardians when you were a child. *Hey, this might sound a little off the subject, or somewhere in left field, but I promise you, if you want to practice living in this truth, without a ton of negative emotions and feelings, you need to be aware of the reason you may have a problem here.*

Don't worry, you're not alone. A lot of us deal with jealous feelings, or we've experienced a few jealous episodes. I remember, after my hubby and I had been working in ministry together for about three years, a woman came into our membership and started working diligently in the church. She was gifted and talented and had all of her gifts and talents on display. A lot of progress was made by her work, which made my hubby ecstatic. But shortly after, I started hearing her name a little too many times.

One night in the parking lot after church, I exploded on my hubby and screamed, *"I'm so sick of hearing that name! So and so this, and so and so that! If I hear that name one more time...!* I jumped into my car and left my hubby standing there with his mouth hanging open. Yes, I know that was very un-First Lady-like behavior, but it goes to show how jealously can rear its ugly head in any of us, no matter our title or position. Yes, jealousy can play a powerful role in a woman not wanting to share her man.

Insecurity. At times you may experience insecurity in your marriage, in your husband's love and respect for you, and in yourself. The easiest way to put this to you is to ask you to look at what security is. Security is: freedom from fear; freedom from doubt; freedom from lack; and freedom from worry. Insecurity causes the opposite: fear, doubt, lack, and worry. Do any of these trigger a major gut-tightening for you? Is your head beating with a vengeance right now? If yes, may I suggest you

Stop, Drop, and Roll

Stop the string of negative thoughts that seem to automatically find fuel.
Drop the bad habit of allowing these kinds of thoughts.
Roll all of these kinds of feelings in a big ole ball, place it into a gigantic slingshot, pull back as hard as you can, and let 'er rip.
Send those feelings and thoughts so deep into space, they can't ever return. Insecurity has no place in your marriage or your life.
Now, we're getting somewhere.

Immaturity. Webster's dictionary defines immaturity as "being
deficient in maturity; lacking wisdom, insight, emotional stability." We are all immature in some areas. However, as does life, your marriage offers periods of growth that need to occur. Your experiences help you to develop trust in your spouse. The more trust you develop, the more secure you are about yourself and your husband. The more secure you are, the more mature you become.

What you focus on will grow, whether good or bad.

When you find yourself traveling down that road of immature behavior or thoughts, begin to talk to yourself about it. Hold only positive words over your mind and your thoughts. You want to focus on the good things—in this case, growth and maturity. Positive self-talk helps, because it steers you in the right direction. Be aware though. It may get a little embarrassing when you have these conversations with yourself out loud. *You may look up one day and to your horror find your hubby staring at you as if you've completely lost your mind.* Yes…this has happened to me.

The bottom line is, you handle immaturity through your pursuit of personal growth, and your determination to put the work in. It may not be easy, but commit to trying. You may find yourself loving the benefits. One of the main things I've learned over my married and relationship life, as have others who've shared with me, is the more mature I am, the better I am able to deal with a lot of the issues that come up. And the ultimate benefit is that my relationships are so much better, and I'm happier and healthier.

Now don't misunderstand me. I'm not condoning a husband who acts like he isn't married, doesn't have family responsibilities, or who hangs out at the club every weekend and all during the week. I'm talking about reasonable and healthy personal time, not *ridiculous and dishonorable.*

If you began to encourage your hubby to spend time with his *homeboys* and do things he enjoys, what do you think will happen? *I mean, really think about it.* When I do that for my hubby, he's a different person. He sees that I trust him. His eyes light up like a little boy who just got a new toy that he didn't expect, like he can't believe I actually told him to go and do what he enjoys. *And that look is priceless!* Let's face it. Men think we want to control them. *And, in a way, we do.* We micro manage them, but only because we love them and care about them, *right?* We just need to loosen the reigns a bit.

Here's a nugget for you. The results of a 2005 United States Nationwide Social Life, Health, and Aging Project study showed that men who do not have enough spare time to spend with their friends or do things they enjoy feel less attracted to their partners, which leads to conflict within their marriages. *Yikes.* That is the last thing you want. It stands to reason that if you encourage him, it may make you more attractive to him—*that's always a plus!*—more caring, more understanding, and more likely to get the things you desire from him.

Aja Smith, author of the *Married Women Rock* marriage blog, suggests, *"Why get upset when he wants to hang out with the guys? There is nothing wrong with a guy hanging out with his friends. Women give men a special type of comfort, but a guy's friends are just different. I'm not saying friends should come first, because we all know your spouse should come before your friends. I'm saying there are certain subject matters that your husband may feel more comfortable discussing with the guys to get a male's opinion. Many guys find relaxation or peace when they hang out with the fellas. Besides, we just need to accept the fact that men and women are made differently, and react differently. Allow your husband to be a man, and don't get mad that he's hanging with the guys."*

She goes on to talk about personal space. *"I've learned it's always good to give your spouse space. I know you married your best friend, and you two are inseparable, but everyone needs time to themselves once and a while. Don't smother your husband so much that you begin to get on his nerves. Give him space so he can miss you. No one is telling you to separate or see someone on the side. I'm telling you to develop your own hobbies and life interests with friends or close family. If he misses you, when he finally sees you, it will be nothing but love."* This my beautiful sister, is *Meeting Your Man's Needs, 101.*

A good wife knows that individual space, pastimes, and friendships are the necessary foundation for relationship health, happiness, and high self-esteem— and that clinginess, jealousy, and neediness will eventually lead to a broken marriage.

One final note

When you think about yourself and the freedom you need to spend time with your sistah-girl friends, to talk, share, vent, or just to get replenished, you must remember that it is no different for your hubby. Your mission as a wife is to make your marriage the best it can be. You want your husband to want to be married to you and to enjoy married life. You don't want him to feel like he is in prison, *or like marriage is something he needs to survive.* You wouldn't want to feel like that, *right?* He values you, so he will not abuse this gift; and if he unintentionally does, just gently remind him. *Granting your husband this freedom will inevitably turn you into his dream mate.*

Red Carpet Reflections

1. Why is it important for your husband to spend time with his friends?

2. How can you handle jealousy, insecurity, and immaturity?

3. What is your greatest takeaway from this chapter?

Chapter Ten

Hubby's #1 Fan and Cheerleader

*"Now I lay me down to sleep,
With megaphone and pom-poms at my feet."*

~Anonymous

Essential Truth #8

When my daughter Shaundrea was nine years old, I enrolled her into the community cheerleader program. She and her cheerleader sisters cheered for The Panthers, the local Pop Warner Football team. I enjoyed watching their routines and supporting them. You may have similar memories with your children. Or, think back to when you were in High School. *I apologize if that is too far to think back, but one thing you can say is that you are blessed to have lived this long!*

So, everyone is in the gym at the basketball game. The girls are in their cute outfits—short skirts, tight tanks, and ankle socks, *designed to make their legs the envy of the entire school's female population.* In their hands are—*you guessed it*—poms poms. The sole purpose of the cheerleading squad is to use specific cheers that build confidence and fire up the players to motivate them to win. Hearing the cheers on the sidelines fuels their belief that they can accomplish their goal.

What do you think would happen if the cheerleaders started criticizing the players in the middle of their game? Do you think that would inspire, or discourage the team? It would surely discourage them, as it would your hubby.

A good wife is her husband's #1 fan and cheerleader. She cheers him on as he strives to win at the game of life and plan the future of his family. *Even though, at times, she might want to look at him as if he has lost his mind and say "For real, that's your plan? You've got to be kidding me. You've got to come better than that,"* a good wife cheers him on when he puts his heart on the table for her and their family.

In his book *Marriage Personalities,* Dr. David Field shares that, "When a wife complains and criticizes, it does not motivate her husband to change." I've seen all too often that many wives have not learned how important it is to be in their husband's corner. No man likes to be doubted or criticized about his ability to lead his family, or anything else for that matter. When you doubt and criticize your hubby, it's like Muhammad Ali punched him right in the gut, knocked the wind out of him, and slam dunked his ego. The result? He shuts down and doesn't want to talk to you at all, retreats and goes deeper into his shell where he becomes even more reluctant to share things with you—*the very thing you don't want to happen.* Then you start to complain about his not having a plan. It creates a vicious and downward spiral.

A good wife thanks her hubby for all he does, expresses her appreciation for his abilities, admires his vision, and feels blessed for his planning. She acknowledges the characteristics that make him stand out to her—his focus, determination, and strength, both physical and emotional—and his diligence and persistence in providing for her and their family. She realizes that men and women are different and acknowledges his manly strengths and the qualities, aptitudes, and actions that complement them with one another. Even something as simple, as appreciating him for retrieving a dish from a shelf too high for her to reach or changing a light bulb, lets him know that she needs, wants, and values him.

What about your husband? Are you cheering him or jeering him? Your hubby's ego is fragile, though he may not show it. Cheering him helps build his confidence and assures him that you believe in him.

Hubby Heart Softeners

There are three powerful keys to your hubby's heart. These important keys are the way to become his advocate, inspire him to be the best he can be, and uplift him.

Key #1 Admire

To admire is "to look upon something or someone with pleasure and wonder"

What do you admire about your husband? What does he do each day that causes you to regard him with awe or admiration? What characteristics or traits does he embody that make your insides do flips when you think about them, or when he demonstrates them?

Your husband needs to be admired by you, just as he needs to be accepted by you. *Admiring is noticing with respect.* Take every opportunity to notice things your hubby does that can be admired. I am sure there are plenty. You just need to pay attention. *Hey, for one he married you!*

Key #2 Affirm

To affirm is "to declare something is true; to strengthen; to approve"

Your hubby craves your affirmations of what he is to you, and what he is in the world. He needs to hear it from you. When he married you, his desire was that you be his #1 supporter; the one who says things to make him feel good, build him, reassure him, and make him feel that he is ok and that what he does passes your test. He wants you to be proud of him. Tell him, *"You are amazing. I love being on this journey with you. I believe in you."*

Cheerleaders root for their team to show their pride in what the team represents. You can do the same for your husband, and you should!

Key #3 Respect

To respect is "to hold in high regard; to be esteemed or honored"

This is a big one. It's so big that I've dedicated extra space to it. *"R-E-S-P-E-C-T, find out what it means to me,"* are the lyrics Aretha Franklin sang in her popular iconic song. The funny thing is that she's asking for respect, and she is a woman. I'm not saying that a woman doesn't want or deserve respect. Of course she does. What I'm saying is that those words relate more to the natural feelings of a man. Respect is the biggest thing for a man, bigger than love, bigger than nurturing.

Do you know that the goal of your hubby is to do the things his heart dreams to do for his wife and children? He dreams of being able to provide for his family, to raise his children in a correct and moral way, so they are a reflection of him, to protect his family and possessions, to advance in his career, to be the greatest lover ever, and to make his wife ecstatically happy. He also dreams that with all his efforts and right intentions, he'll receive the respect that he thinks he fully deserves as a man.

If you follow only one scripture in the bible on the principles of marriage, let it be this one:

> *"...Wives honor or respect your husbands."*
> ~Ephesians 5:33

In the book, *Love and Respect: Motivating Your Man God's Way*, Dr. Emerson Eggerichs says that respect is the secret to a wife's cracking the code of her husband's deepest need. He goes on to say that when a husband feels disrespected, he feels the message from his wife is she doesn't accept, approve, or respect him as a man, husband or human being. These feelings cause him to shut down and close off his spirit.

When I read about this, it was such an enlightening moment for me. I had learned that men need respect, but my understanding didn't kick in all the way until I read

Dr. Eggerich' comparison of the way a man feels when he is disrespected with the way a woman feels when her husband tells her that she's fat, or needs to lose some weight, or needs to go to the gym. *Yikes*. That really brought it home. Two things you never mention to a woman are her sagging breasts and her weight!

Women were made to love and nurture, what Dr. Eggerichs calls our "mother language," the language we are born to understand. Respect is your husband's mother language. It's how men are made.

A few years ago my husband and I facilitated a workshop called "Man Speak/Woman Speak: Understanding and Interpreting the Languages of the Sexes." We pointed out the many differences in the way men and women communicate, their social behaviors, their interpretation of experiences, and their basic needs. For example: boys are taught to be strong, analytical, and grounded; girls are taught to use their imagination and be creative; boys are taught not to show too much emotion or tenderness; girls are taught to talk about the things in their hearts; men should make direct requests; women should put others' needs above their own; men need respect; women need love. Of these, love and respect topped the list.

Dr. John Gottman, a leading authority on marriage, studied two thousand couples over a period of twenty years. In his book *Why Marriages Succeed or Fail*, he explained that no matter what style of marriage the couples' adopted, their discussions—*for the most part*—carry a strong undercurrent of two basic ingredients, love and respect. Men need to be respected as much as women need to be loved. One thing my hubby always says is that a man hates to see his words fall to the ground. Translation: if your hubby is important to you, and he expresses something important to him, you need to do your part in listening and helping him with what he asks of you. This shows respect. His plans and foresight are for you.

Being your hubby's #1 fan and cheerleader is your godly assignment. Just as when you were in school, and you had assignments that you were responsible to complete, you have assignments to complete regarding your husband. He deeply desires you to be alright with the things he plans, because his basic need is to make you happy. He desires to make you proud of him—*which brings me to reiterate something here*. Please do not turn your nose up, make ugly faces, or smack your lips when he shares his plans with you. He *needs* you. Remember, his strength of vision is to see in the distance and plan ahead; he's the big picture guy. Your strength of vision is to see up close and catch the details; you're the details gal. You do what you do best, so he can do what he does best. Don't point out negative details about your hubby, unless you want him to start pointing out negative details about you!

Trust me when I tell you that opportunities will present themselves for you to offer suggestions that may better fit his vision. If he respects and loves you, he values your opinion. But don't use that against him and try to manipulate him. Use the acronym O-W-N in these situations; comment o*nly when necessary,* and always strive to do it in love. This may be a little tough, because you may think that you know more, or your plan is better. For the health of your marriage, *please resist the urge.* You will thank me—*and yourself*—later.

A good wife knows that her strength lies in her support of her husband, that her love is his source of inspiration, and that her eyes and words for him are his affirmation of success in being the best man he can be.

One final note:

Your hubby is your teammate, so you need to keep rooting for him, to show him your undying support. Remember the 2011 playoffs? Yes, I know you have to think pretty far back. The Lakers got embarrassed because they didn't act like teammates and didn't support each other. To a man, one of the worst things in the world is seeing that his wife doesn't believe in him. So, get your pom-poms out and Rah, Rah, Rah for your man!

Red Carpet Reflections

1. What happens when a wife complains and criticizes her husband?

2. List 3 powerful keys to your husband's heart.

3. What is your greatest takeaway from this chapter?

Chapter Eleven

Hubby, Knight, Superman

*"Everybody's searching for a hero. People need someone to look up to.
I never found anyone to fulfill my needs."*

~The Greatest Love of All

Essential Truth #9

A hero is someone noted for courageous acts or nobility of character, the traits found in both Superman and Knights, in or out of their shining armor. Some wives have a tendency to look in all the wrong places for their heroes, but a good wife looks no farther than her own marriage. She knows that her hubby can be her Knight and her Superman, if she *accepts* him for who he is and what he's good at. Even though she might want to compare him to other men and think, '*Dang, he's so sorry! He can't do anything I need him to!* Or, *What do I need him for?*' she knows to accept his limitations, whatever they might be, and focus on the positive.

The United States Secret Service, a federal law enforcement agency under the U.S. Department of Homeland Security, protects and ensures the safety of our nation's current and former leaders, such as the President, Vice President, past presidents, presidential candidates, visiting heads of states, and foreign embassies and their families. In the same spirit of protection, a knight is an elite warrior with responsibilities to protect the King's army—*even at the risk of his own life.* Chivalry, noble-mindedness, exceptional politeness, and attentiveness toward women were the primary traits of medieval knights. They represented an overall system of proper conduct, which extended beyond the battlefield into everyday life. The motto they lived by was, *Always treat a lady with respect and defend her against any danger.*

These are also traits of your hubby when he acts as your knight. His duty is to protect you, and he doesn't take that duty lightly. My hubby and I went sailing one afternoon with my sister and her husband, and after we returned and were safely off the boat, he told me that he'd been totally stressed out during the entire adventure. He had been constantly thinking, *"How will I save my wife if something happens while we're out here in this ocean?"* I was shocked. I had no idea those thoughts had been running through his mind and heart. That let me know how serious my protection is to him. Then I recalled that when we were first married, he told me anything could be compromised, except my safety. *Wow.*

Your hubby is commanded by God in Ephesians 5:33 to love you. This command requires him to demonstrate the highest level of respect for you, care for you to the best of his knowledge, and protect you to the best of his abilities, even if it means to risk his own safety, or his life. Protecting you fills him with pride, power, and confidence, medicine for his soul. To him, protecting you is as natural as breathing.

Your hubby is also your Superman, your Super Hero. Superman has a rescuer's spirit that drives him to want to save humanity from the bad guys. He possesses great strength, care, compassion, and love. Just as Superman embodies strength, care, compassion, and love, so does your hubby, and he is born with a spirit to rescue you. He shows this by always offering solutions to your problems, whether you ask him or not. Superman is also very handsome. It's ok if some people don't think your husband is handsome. Remember, beauty is in the eyes of the beholder!

Superman craves appreciation and affirmation from the people he saves, and it makes him want to do even more. Superman's only weakness is kryptonite; radioactive meteorites from his home planet that render him powerless and poison him. All one needs to do to defeat him is direct some kryptonite at him. You may not always see heroic traits in your hubby. Maybe your disapproval, dissatisfaction, down talking, negative attitude, and lack of belief in him has been his kryptonite, poisoning his spirit and killing his desire to want to please you. Hopefully that is not the case, but if so, this is your chance to right your wrong and look for the heroic qualities in him.

Your hubby craves your approval, appreciation, and affirmation, and receiving them drives him to want to do more for you. Do you know how important it is to your husband to know that you appreciate all the things he does for you and your family? He works hard to show you he loves you, so show him that you love him too. *How?* Not by scowling, or looking sour, but by looking sincerely pleased and finding positive things about him.

It's in the Details. Most women pay close attention to details. It's part of our gift from God. Men were the hunter gatherers, designed to see far off in the distance, so they could bring home the food—and see far into the future, so they could plan for your security and prosperity. Women were the nesters, homemakers, and child caretakers, designed to see the details up close. But I think we've gotten into a bad habit of paying attention to negative details more than positive ones in our husbands—especially after we've been married for a few years. *They* say that after two years, the honeymoon phase is over and we stop noticing the good and start focusing on the bad in our marriage, and in our husbands. Does this sound a bit familiar? Hey, more truth.

If this describes you, don't feel bad. Try this. List ten wonderful and exciting things to compliment your hubby on. Go beyond the usual *"I love how you dress," "I love your height,"* and *"I love how your muscles bulge when you lift something heavy,"* although that last one's not a bad one. Get intimate and thoughtful with things you don't usually compliment him on. Be sincere, and talk from your heart. I love giving my hubby compliments like this:

"I love the way your eyes sparkle and light up when you have an exciting idea to share with me."
"I love how your brows furrow when you are in deep thought."
"I love how when you smile that crooked smile; it sends chills up my spine."
"I love the way your love radiates right through your fingertips when the love you have for me is on your mind."
"I love how your smile is so genuine and spreads across your entire face when I tell you what a great lover you are."

Compliment him *often* to let him know you appreciate who he is and what he does. Afterward, witness for yourself what it does for him. If you can't dive right into the intimate areas, here are seven additional suggested areas to compliment your hubby on, to make him feel like he is your Superman.

1. Physical appearance
2. Gifts, talents, skills and abilities
3. Handyman-ness
4. How sexy he looks in certain attire, *i.e. your apron*
5. Character traits, like funny, solid, strong
6. Spiritual leadership –he prays for you
7. Sexual prowess

This is so important, that it bears repeating. Compliment your hubby. Tell him he's a great lover; tell him he's the best; tell him he's strong and sexy and he makes you feel good. Tell him he's your king.

A good wife knows to find the abilities of her Superman and the traits of her Knight in her hubby and let him know that she sees them, how great he is at them, and how much she appreciates him for them.

One final note

Men are inspired by their wives. All they want to do is please us. If he is not the most athletic man, but he's an excellent math teacher, great with numbers, and has the ability to mentally add the prices on your grocery list, let him know that you notice and appreciate that skill. Just don't ask him to run up and down the basketball court, high fly, and slam dunk like Kobe Bryant, or run the marathon! Simply say, *"Baby, get your cape and teach that addition, multiplication, or standard deviation!"*

To this point I have shared with you *9 Truths and Other Marriage Essentials*. Now, I will share a powerful ingredient that will boost your confidence and endear your hubby to you more deeply emotionally and physically, *which is just where you want him to be.*

Red Carpet Reflections

1. List 3 traits of Knights and Superman that describe your husband.

2. List 3 compliments you can give your husband.

3. What is your greatest takeaway from this chapter?

Chapter Twelve

Hubby's Fun, Sexy, Classy Wife

"Good things come in threes."
~ Author Unknown

Essential Truth #10

As a little girl, I loved to play outside, climb trees and fences, play dodge ball, kick ball, and chase, and participate in all kinds of sports. Maybe this was you too. Unfortunately, as we become more '*seasoned,*' life starts to interfere with our sense of play and—*more than we want to admit*—we forget about having fun altogether. A fundamental factor in a women's ability to create and maintain a happy marriage is the ability to maintain her childlike quality of playfulness. One way I know this childlike quality is still in me is my love for watching cartoons. I love the Flintstones and watch them every night! This reassures me that I'm not taking myself too seriously. No one wants to spend time with an insufferable bore.

In Chapter 3, Self-Knowledge First, All Others Second, I shared the value of self-love and self-discovery, and that they are inside jobs. Sexiness is also an inside job. Sexy is a state of mind, a state of being. Think about it. Have you ever saw a woman walk into a room, or cross your path, who had a sexy confidence that you and others couldn't help but notice, and you found yourself staring at her? Even if her body wasn't perfect, or far from it, the energy she had made her sexy? The sexier you believe you are, the sexier you are. Belief is very powerful.

Just as a sense of play adds a special quality to a woman and her marriage, sexiness adds to a woman's confidence and attractiveness, brings out her *inner Queen*, and has a revitalizing and stimulating effect on her hubby and her marriage. Now, look at yourself in the mirror. What part of you is sexiest? It might be the way you open your eyes big and wide. It might be the way you walk when you strut across the kitchen preparing dinner or a snack for your hubby. Whatever it is, find your sexy, and then work it!

Another result of knowing your *inner Queen* is inner confidence. Inner confidence, without boasting or intentionally drawing attention to yourself, shows class. Classiness simply means that you know how to carry yourself, with quiet confidence and grace. You know when and when not to voice your opinion, in public and in private. You know which tone of voice to use to nurture and soothe, and which to use when you're meeting your husband's co-workers, associates, or boss. It means you don't embarrass yourself, or your hubby. Classy confidence is ageless. It's slightly understating your power in a way that lets people see that you know who you are, but don't need to prove it. It shows that you know you are beautiful inside, and out.

As a Fun, Sexy, and Classy wife you know that you can—*and should*—flirt shamelessly with your husband. Think back to when you were dating, or back to the first few years after you were married. Most of you flirted with your husband because your love and romance was still fresh and new. I suggest you revisit those memories, *and on a frequent basis*. Even if you didn't flirt with your husband back then, there is no better time to start than now. In case your memory is a bit foggy in the flirt game, just playfully tease your husband, with the intention to place—and keep—yourself on his mind, with the promise of something to come.

Here are a few tips to get you started.

- ➤ Make eye contact, with sexy confidence. *This is your husband we're talking about*, so it's ok to be playful, take a few risks, try out some new looks (*in the mirror first*), and don't worry about anything. Remember, you are trying to convey a message with your eyes! But don't stare. This will make him uncomfortable. *Try this: Imagine your hubby is a few feet away from you and you look at him until he looks at you. You look for a few seconds with your sexy confident look, then look off, then look back. Notice how he responds.*

- Hug your hubby for no less than ten seconds. Feel your body press into his; feel your energy go into him (*this may take a little longer than ten seconds, but it's all good*).
- Hold and caress his hands tenderly and erotically. *Erotic* simply means arousing sexual feelings or desires. Remember back in the day when guys use to rub the middle of a female's hand in a circle when they wanted to go to second base? While you caress his hand, let some erotic thoughts run through your mind. What you are thinking will transfer through your touch as you caress him. Your husband *will* notice, and he *will* be enticed.
- Use pet names or terms of endearment to address your hubby, but be sure it's something he'll be comfortable with and play along with. Don't try to act like Olive Oil and say *"Heeeyyy Popeye,"* batting your eyes, expecting him to respond. He'll most likely look at you like you're crazy if he doesn't play those kinds of games.

- Learn to say, "*I love you,*" or "*You are the sexiest man in the universe,*" or "*Kiss me,*" in another language—preferably French. *Try this: Practice saying in French "I love you, my darling"—"Je t'aime mon chéri."* Come on Queen, get your French accent on!
- Kiss your husband often; either a peck on the lips, cheek, neck, or softly on the eyelids, and let it linger. Or use your imagination. Take some time to surprise him with a deep French kiss to really give him something to remember.

Here are a few more fun, sexy, and classy tips:

- ✓ *Be bold and courageous. Express your sensuality and sexiness.* This is God's gift to you and your man.
- ✓ *Take some risks. Try some new things.* Plan a romantic getaway to somewhere you've never been before and promise your hubby a surprise. Your surprise might include initiating lovemaking, giving him a massage, washing his hair, playing romantic games, loving on him for his exclusive pleasure (*yes, I did write that!*), or wearing sexy lingerie to entice him and give him something to see and enjoy. Men are visual creatures, created to admire and desire us.
- ✓ *Be uninhibited.* This is simply a byproduct of being in touch and in tune with your own body and aware

of how your five senses are stimulated by sight, sound, touch, taste, and smell.
- ✓ *Dance.* Dancing is sensual, erotic, freeing, spiritual, and loving. Take a class. Free your mind. Love your body. Free your spirit.
- ✓ *Picture your hubby in sexy terms.* This will surely bring the sexiness out in you. Hear the sound of his voice and how it moves you or wakes up erotic feelings in you.
- ✓ *Delight in him*…how his skin feels, how his touch feels on you, or how his natural scent or fragrance smells. Daydream about his physical features. Use your imagination.

What if you don't feel confident doing any of these? One thing is certain; in order to become comfortable doing all of these, you will need to develop a certain level of confidence. Unfortunately, most women have been through so much drama in their lives and have had their self-esteem pummeled so many times that their confidence is buried. Fortunately, there are so many ways to learn to uncover your confidence and build it back up. I have a ton of tips, but unless you take action, apply them in your life, and keep practicing, you'll remain in the same place you might be right now—*on your personal hamster wheel.* And that's no fun.

Before you read any further, make this declaration right now:

Today is the day I release my confidence from being held hostage. Today I set it free. Today I make a commitment to cross the bridge to get to the other side. Today I step into becoming the confident, sexy, classy, and fun wife my hubby craves.

Now, for some Powerful Confidence Building Tips. Are you ready? Here we go!

5 Powerful Ways to Build Self-Confidence

- *Speak it into existence.* Every morning when you wake up, find the nearest mirror. Look yourself straight in the eyes and recite with conviction and assurance, Psalms 139:14:
  "I will praise you O God for I am fearfully and wonderfully made." Then, say, *"I love you. I really love you."*

Do this consistently for 21 days and watch your opinion of yourself change.

- *Make four lists about yourself: strengths, achievements, talents/skills, what you admire or value about yourself.* Most women have not taken the time to think about these areas and may have the false belief that this was selfish, or a waste of time. Not true! It's time to change your mind-set and do it. We all have strengths, gifts, talents, and skills. We have all achieved something, even if it's birthing your child—*a monumental task might I add.* We all have things we admire or value about ourselves. Here is your opportunity to take some time to examine yourself. You may be surprised what you discover about You.

- ❖ *Groom yourself and dress yourself with clothes that flatter, not flaunt or hide.* When I groom myself and get my hair, nails, and feet pampered and eyebrows arched, I feel like a Super Star. Just seeing my reflection reminds me of how much I care about myself. This is directly related to self-esteem and self-love, two sides of the same coin and an important step in building self-confidence. Selecting—*and wearing*—clothes that accentuate your assets and best features takes the focus away from your less than desirable parts. Yes, we all have them. And definitely do not wear clothes so tight that your breasts squeeze out and topple over. *That is not sexy.*
- ❖ *Change a small habit.* Set all the gigantic ambitious goals in your mind aside and start small with something that you know you can do: drinking a bottle of water when you wake up; waking up 15-20 minutes earlier; or jotting things down, so you'll

remember. When I wanted to stop drinking so much coffee and drink more tea, I substituted just one cup of coffee per week with tea. Gradually, I made it two days per week, then three. I felt so proud that I was able to do it. Yes, we all have visions of grandeur on accomplishing major goals, but the best way to feel accomplished is to take many small steps, which add up to major steps. This is success. And more success leads to more self-confidence.

❖ *Kill negative thoughts and replace them with positive thoughts.* To kill something means to make it not exist, or make it not give you any more trouble. The difference between killing negative thoughts and killing a bug is that the bug will not come back to bother you, but the negative thoughts try to come back again and again. Having a spray can full of positive thoughts is necessary to counteract the negative ones. Thoughts come from our feelings, experiences, and emotions. While you're killing negative thoughts in your mind, you're placing new positive thoughts in your mind at the same time. Positive thoughts act as kryptonite to negative thoughts that bombard you daily.

Building self-confidence is an on-going learning process. In the midst of learning, I'd find myself rushing around, speeding, zipping, and walking aggressively. I did the same with my thoughts. I'd labeled myself an over thinker. When I caught myself doing that, I'd say, *"Slow down. Confident women don't rush around. Confident women don't live out of their head. They live from their bodies and from their senses."* This positive self-talk did wonders for my self-confidence. I became aware of what I was doing and was able to make a simple adjustment to correct my behavior, and gained more confidence in the process.

A good wife knows that she must take time to nurture and give to herself and take the highest care of her body, mind, and spirit. A high self-care factor automatically results in a more confident, classy, sexy, fun wife and a dynamic, attractive partner to her hubby.

One final thought

Keeping the right balance is key to keep your hubby's heart aflame. Just as you know when to throw another log onto the fire to ignite more flames, it's important to know when to be more *Fun, Sexy, and Classy,* to keep the flames burning in your hubby. If you keep these tips and thoughts close to your heart and in the forefront of your mind, and practice them daily, the *Fun, Sexy, Classy You* is bound to come busting out. These key elements will add spark to your self-esteem, spice to your relationship, and sizzle to your marriage! ☺

Are you still with me? You're on the home stretch. Here come my final two essential truths. Ready? Let's go!

Red Carpet Reflections

1. List 3 tips that bring out the *Fun, Sexy, and Classy* in you.

2. List 3 powerful tips that build self-confidence.

3. What is your greatest takeaway from this chapter?

Part Four
Let's Talk About Sex

Chapter Thirteen

Your Ultimate Marriage Power Tool
Sex

"Sex is a wonderful experience between husband and wife that provides physical, emotional, and spiritual bonding."

~Focus on the Family

Psalms 139: 14 says, "I will praise you O God, for I am fearfully and wonderfully designed." Part of that design is your human sexuality; something that is necessary to attract and be attracted to the opposite sex. Unfortunately, many religious organizations and society have perpetuated negative messages over the centuries, about sex and sexuality. Fortunately, I will help clear things up with the following Sex Truths.

Sex Truth #1
God Gave the Gift of Sex to Married Couples for Pleasure

Power
Strength and energy, force might; ability or capacity to do something; to inspire, spur, sustain; to fuel, supply force to operate.

Tool
Anything used as a means of accomplishing a task or purpose.

Truths
Verified or indisputable facts, propositions, principles, or the like.

My husband loves power tools. Why? Because power tools make everything easier and manual labor a thing of the past. We love the word *easier*, don't we? Even when it comes to sex. Does sex make your marriage easier? *Yes, in the areas it is supposed to.* There will still be work involved in making your marriage successful, but sex can make communication, respect, pleasing, and satisfying each other easier. Sex definitely makes for a happier, healthier, more fun, exciting, and interesting marriage. *You just gotta know how important sex is to your marriage. And you just gotta know that God gave the gift of sex to married couples for pleasure.*

Salt n Pepa, a Grammy Award winning all female rap group, sang *"Let's Talk About Sex,"* and a good wife can sing right along, because she knows how important her sexual relationship is to her hubby and tries her best not to deny him. *Even though she might want to turn her back to him, pull the covers up to her chin, roll her eyes with an attitude, think 'Not again,' smack her lips, or tell him she has a headache*, she doesn't do any of that, because she knows that sex is important to her husband and that it should be just as important to her.

I know there are times when you are just not feeling it—*but all the time?* One thing you should remember is that sex is the tool most husbands need to connect emotionally to their wives. They place such a high value on this connection that when you turn them down, you crush their ability to connect and bond with you, *not to mention their egos*. To your husband, your desire for a healthy sex life shows him that you love him. Women need to be nurtured, protected, and cared for, to feel loved. Men need a sexual connection with their women, to feel loved and nurtured. I know, it feels kind of backward, but that's the way it works.

As irritating as it may be for some wives, you should listen to what your husband tells you about the way men think. In his mind and heart, he believes you don't love him if you don't want to make love with him. He longs to be desired by you. BELIEVE IT!

To help make this easier and really work for you, I'll share two *additional power tools* that will help you embrace this precious and valuable area of your marriage. They are Mindset and Speaking Up.

Mindset

What is mindset? It is a set way you think about any specific topic or area of life. Your mind is like an air traffic controller, acting as the command center for planes and pilots. Whatever the controller tells them to do, they do. Your body will do whatever your mindset tells it to do. If your mind is not set in a way that stirs up sexual desire for your hubby, you can learn how to shift it.

If you think of lovemaking as a chore, a duty, or something to be dreaded, begin by looking at it differently. Look at it as the pleasure gift God gave to husbands and wives. If your first thought is to reject your husband and his advances, just try saying yes instead, like this, *"Ok, give me a minute."* Then go shower, take a bath, or whatever you need to do. And invite him to do the same. While you're getting ready, focus your mind on how your lovemaking is a pleasure gift. Breathe a few deep cleansing breaths to place yourself in the moment. Shift your mindset from past memories and feelings to future thoughts and to-do's. This really works. Your mind is powerful, and with practice you can direct it.

Recall other times when you connected intimately with your husband, or think about the favorite thing you like him to do for you. Visualizing is amazingly powerful. It sears images into your mind. Use your imagination, and create the images you want to experience. You'll be surprised what kind of mood this puts you in. Your husband bears everything about himself when he comes to you for sex and lovemaking. His entire emotional being is wrapped up in his need for your sexual attention. In his eyes, rejecting his advances is rejecting him and all he is as a man, a husband, and a human being. You do not want to ever do that. If you need help in this area, I can help.

Speaking Up

An equally effective power tool used to enhance your sexual connection with your hubby is: Speaking up. To delight in his advances, you need to know what delights you, and make sure he knows too. Many women have a problem with sex, because they are not enjoying it and are not being satisfied. If someone asked you if your hubby does his best to satisfy you sexually, what would your answer be? Would it be an absolute *YES?* A hesitant *Sometimes?* An *Uh, kinda?* Or a resounding *No!*

If your answer is one of the last three, you are not alone. However, you must ask the question, "Why?" Unfortunately, our society makes us think that men know it all when it comes to sex, but truth be told, they know what makes them feel good, but many have hardly a clue how to make a woman feel good.

If you have ever seen porno flicks (*I'm a Believer but haven't always known Christ* ☺)*,* you know that what the actors do is very unrealistic. You know that one longing look in your husband's eyes doesn't suddenly make you ready to *do the do*. One touch or grab of a body part doesn't automatically *make you ready for a romp*. And throwing you on the bed doesn't instantly fill you with hot passion. No, none of that is real. It takes a whole lot more to get you aroused and ready.

If you know that, are you communicating with him about it? Are you sharing with him what you need and what you love? If not, how would he know? *Despite what you may think, he is not a mind reader.* What you expect him to know and do, he probably doesn't and won't. So, do you keep quiet and suffer in silence, letting the frustration, resentment and dissatisfaction build to the point when you don't want to have sex with your husband? Or, do you learn what to say and how to speak up for what you want your hubby to know about you, your body, your sexual desires, and your needs?

In a scene in *Star Trek 2,* Lt. Slavak, asks Captain James Tiberious Kirk for permission to speak freely. Captain Kirk replies that self-expression is not one of her problems. Like Lt. Slavak, we know how to speak freely in many areas of our life. When we want our kids to clean up their room, when we go out with friends after work, when we have coffee dates, when we go shopping for a pair of cute shoes we love, and even when we start a business, we say what we want and what we are looking for. But when it comes to getting our sexual needs met it's a whole other ball game. *Why is that?*

Many of us have been taught from a very early age that sex talk is taboo, off limits, something good girls don't talk about, or something the man is in charge of and knows how to do.

Sometimes we hear good things about it, then we hear bad things about it, and get confused and don't know what to think. But the truth is that you need to talk about it. You need to speak up. You must communicate your needs to your husband.

A good wife knows that changing her mindset and communicating her desires are two of the most important parts of getting her sexual needs met and enjoying love-making to the fullest.

One final note

It's not only important to talk about it, but to learn about it, and be about it. When you speak up it boosts your confidence and encourages you to speak more. Kick all the blocks and barriers out of the way and don't let them rob you of experiencing the joy of this monumental gift.

Red Carpet Reflections

1. List 2 power tools that help you embrace the gift of sex in your marriage.

2. Explain why these two power tools are so important.

3. What is your greatest takeaway from this chapter

Chapter Fourteen

Seven Sexual Power Tools
Plug In and Practice

"Work with whatever power tools you may have at your command."
~Anonymous

Sex Truth #2
God Wants You to Enjoy Sex with Your Husband

You know just as men have power tools, women do too. Speaking freely is Lt. Slavak's *power tool*. Wouldn't it be fantastic if we all used that power tool? God wants you to use that power tool so you can learn to enjoy your sexual life with your husband. If you're like millions of women, you may be shy or extremely uncomfortable talking to him about this subject. So, I've put together a list of *Seven Sexual Power Tools that help you Communicate Your Desires to Your Husband*. See which ones speak to you.

1. *Know it.* The better you know yourself, the better able you will be to share your knowledge with your husband. One of the main reasons most women don't express their needs and desires with their husbands is because they don't have a clue what they are. Getting to know yourself increases self-awareness, self-acceptance, self-love, and self-confidence. There is nothing more empowering than knowing yourself.
2. *Read it.* Read a steamy novel or magazine article to your hubby that contains things you would like to try. Don't be turned off by this suggestion. Just reading something that excites you, stimulates you, or sparks your imagination, can be extremely freeing. After a few minutes of nervousness, you may be surprised at how easy and comfortable you become. *Don't knock it 'til you try it.*
3. *Write it.* If you're dying to express your needs or desires to your hubby, but can't seem to say the words, write the words. Write about what makes you feel good sexually, how you like to be touched, kissed, and caressed. Always start your communication with a compliment and precede it with whatever your term of endearment is, i.e., *Baby, Honey, Sweetie, Big Daddy*, etc., then "*When we're making love, I really like it when you…*" Or, "*It feels so good to me when you…*"

Or, *"I love how you...."* I have done this on a few occasions, and I can testify that it works.

4. *Code it.* Come up with code words that tells your hubby you are *ready for love*. This is a fun creative way to alleviate the pressure of *sex talk*. You can think of things you like, or things that come naturally to you and turn them into playful code words. If you're a student you can say, *"I want you to do some homework tonight."* If you like sailing, you can say, *"I want to take a ride on your speed boat."* If you like gardening you can say, *"Come and plant some fruit in my garden."*

5. *Speak it (outside of the bedroom).* Open your mouth. If your hubby is doing something that you just don't like, you must bring it up *outside of the bedroom*. If you need to start by sharing how uncomfortable or nervous you are about bringing up the subject, then do that. Is it scary and embarrassing? *Yes.* Does just the thought of speaking up make your stomach churn and do flip-flops? *Yes.* But that's your sign that it's time to push past your comfort zone and do something different. It's time to grow and learn to enjoy the gift of sex that God has given to you and your hubby.

6. *Say it (inside the bedroom).* This may make you cringe, but it will be the best thing you can ever

do for your sexual satisfaction. For example, if your hubby is using too much pressure on any area of your body, you can gently say, *"a little softer."* That simple. And if your hubby is doing something that you like and are truly enjoying, you can say, *"Mmmm…"* or *"Oooh…,"* like you're enjoying a rich creamy piece of chocolate. Doesn't that sound delicious? Think how it will sound to your hubby.

7. *Move it.* Touch is just as powerful as words. Sometimes, just by gently moving his hand, pressing on it for more pressure, lifting it for less pressure, or turning it—and *oohing* as you do, to let him know he's doing even better, is the magic tool that lets him know that you care about feeling good. He wants to know you're in it with him. He wants to please you. He wants the best for you! So don't be afraid to lovingly, gently move him to show him what you like.

Right here, I will share a very personal story with you. I am very serious about making my marriage enjoyable, sexy, and fun, so I read a lot and try a lot of the things I learn about. I learned I should be direct when I ask my man what he likes, so there's no misunderstanding. Well, I did one night, and our discussion went something like this.

> *"So what are your expectations for tonight?"* I asked.
>
> *"Who are you supposed to be?"* He looked at me funny.
>
> *"What do you mean?"* I asked, not understanding.
>
> *"You sounded like a woman of the night."*
>
> *What??!!* *"I was just trying to find out what you wanted. And that was supposed to be my sexy voice."*
>
> *"No, uh uh; don't ever use that voice or ask me that again"*, shaking his head.
>
> *"Ugh!"* Shaking *my* head.

Imagine my embarrassment after that little episode. But I didn't let that stop me. I just took a deep breath and pushed on like he hadn't said anything!

Everything that we do may not work the first time—*or at all*—but we must try, and keep trying. So be courageous. Your hubby will be happy you care that much about your sexual relationship with him, and he will applaud your effort. Remember, pleasing you is his number one priority. It gives him confidence beyond belief.

Utilize these Sexual Power Tools so you both can experience maximum pleasure each time you come together. Making love to one another means exactly that. You are *creating love in your relationship, making more love together.*

Power Up

When I first decided to use *Power Tools* to explain these Essential Sex Truths as your ultimate marriage power tools, I had no clue how so many were relatable to sex in your marriage. My *Power Tools* knowledge began and ended with saws and sanders. Maybe yours does too. If so, it's time to expand your knowledge. Here are a few "tools" you and your hubby can experiment with next time you're ready to *power up*. Keep in mind these terms are used as metaphors.

- ❖ *The Impact Driver:* applies downward, rotational "torque." This is self-explanatory. Your imagination may have just shifted into gear.
- ❖ *The Radial Arm Saw:* designed to make accurate cross cuts. Use it for cutting evil tricks, devices, and thoughts right out of the mind and out of the bedroom, or wherever you make whoopee.
- ❖ *The Rotary Tool*: a multitasker that drills, polishes, grinds, and engraves. Your hubby can learn to caress and suck your breasts, while simultaneously attending to your

divine garden (*women aren't the only ones who can multitask!*).

- *The Belt Sander:* removes old finishes and smoothes out rough edges. With practice, this tool helps smooth out the surfaces and rough edges of your hubby's techniques. (*Did I just write that? Yes I did.*)
- *The Heat Gun:* helps loosen old paint and thaw out 'frozen' pipes. Sometimes hardened attitudes and frostbite have settled on your passion. This powerful tool lets you put heat on them and melt them all away.
- *The Scroll Saw:* has a blade that reciprocates. It takes two to tangle. No one-sided action going on here.

A note about hygiene

Before you and your hubby come together for lovemaking, be sure you both clean yourselves (soap and water preferably) from top, including your mouth and tongue, to bottom, and every crack and crevice in between. A fishy vagina, a pissy penis, or a smelly butt crack is not attractive, appealing, or sexy. *And that's real talk.*

A good wife knows that healthy, monogamous sexual pleasure is a gift God gave to her and her husband that seals the bond of love and distinguishes them as marital love partners, not just friends. She holds that gift like a treasure and commits to the fullest use of it.

One final note:

It's time to make sex fun again. After reading the above list, my hope is that your knowledge and anticipation have increased and that you become an avid *Power Tools Wife*. And don't just try once and stop. *Practice, practice, practice!*

As with anything you learn, you should keep at it and be determined that you are going to master it. And, by all means, learn to relax and enjoy yourself—*and your husband*.

Red Carpet Reflections

1. List 3 sexual power tools that communicate your desires to your husband.

2. List 3 *Power Up* power tools you can experiment with your husband.

3. What is your greatest takeaway from this chapter?

Part Five
Get On
Your Grind

Chapter Fifteen

Do the Work

"Work is victory! Get busy and work with all of your might!"

~ Ralph Waldo Emerson

You have just successfully completed reading all the sex truths, and other marriage essentials every good wife knows! Congratulations! Now, it's time to learn to sharpen your skills through application and practice.

Dennis Kimbro, author of the #1 best-selling book *Think and Grow Rich: A Black Choice,* says *"Success in anything worthwhile is the result of whole-hearted faith, tremendous persistence, and work—steady, unremitting, conscientious work!"*

Webster's definition of work is *"any effort directed to produce or accomplish something; to bring about any result by work, effort, or action."*

I love to dance. I have always loved to dance. Recently, I had the opportunity to perform a dance I had dreamed of doing for quite a few years. When I made the decision to dance, I had only three weeks to practice. Imagine a seasoned sistah who hadn't performed a dance in over five years. On top of that, I had stiffness, crackling bones, and decreased memory. *'What was that move again?'* I started out a little shaky, but as time went on, and as I practiced—*even when I didn't feel like it,* I found myself getting better and better, becoming more confident, and *feeling* the dance, instead of *thinking* about it.

We were two weeks into practice and rehearsing when the choreographer commented on how much progress I had made in such a short time. She surmised that I had really been putting in some work. She was right. I did put the work in, and as a result, I performed at such a high level that I surprised myself! My choreographer said I *sold* the dance. That happened because I had made a commitment to work as hard as I could and as much as was necessary. I was so proud of myself. I felt I had accomplished something phenomenal, and I knew that I was responsible for my success. It will be the same for you, once you commit to do your work.

Success will not happen overnight. As Mr. Kimbro tells us, *"Anything worth its salt will take some effort on your part."* So, what work will you have to put in, to apply the steps in this book into your daily life and reap the highest reward?

1. First—*and most important*—know and remember that your mind can be your greatest ally, *or your greatest enemy*. What you believe is everything. Like the air traffic controller, you are the controller of your mind. It will do what you tell it to. So, transform your mind. Determine what thoughts and beliefs you want to feed it, so that you can think what you *want* to think. Think on things that are *good*. Think on the growth that will come when you practice the information shared here.
2. Next, tell your mind that you love, honor, and cherish your marriage and your husband so much that you are willing to try new ways of thinking, behaving, and whatever else is needed to preserve, strengthen, and grow your marriage.
3. Then you must *sow* all of this information and intention deep in your heart, wholeheartedly *meditate* on it, and *commit* to break out of old ways and begin anew.
4. Lastly, you must persevere and persist. There will be times when you will want to quit or

shelve your effort. When that happens, remember your goal, remember why you started, and remember how you want to finish.

One final note

To get maximum results from your work in this chapter, you will need to complete the home assignments listed in the next chapter. Remember to apply what you learn through practice, practice, and more practice. Repetition *is* the mother or learning.

Chapter Sixteen

Rewards Program

"The one element that makes your results unique is You."

~ M. McKnight

A rewards program is designed to provide additional benefits to its customers. In the same manner I have designed this rewards program specifically for you. To help you have the highest success from your learning and application of the steps, tips, and tools shared throughout this book, I have created a few home exercises.

Home Exercises

- ❖ *Essentials & Truths:* Add at least one of the fourteen into your daily life each week.
- ❖ *Getting to know yourself:* Apply at least two tips into your life each week.

- *Flirting tips:* Choose at least one flirting tip to practice weekly or monthly; it's your choice.
- *Pick one night:* This week or next week—*but no later than that*—take a warm bubble bath and relax. Bathe yourself in scented oils or lotions. Fix yourself up; do your hair and make-up, and put on a cute nighty, a lounge outfit, or some lingerie. Then sit or snuggle with your hubby and watch a movie, listen to music, or—*like Jill Scott says*—just be silent.
- *Enjoy the experience with no goal or expectations:* If you have children, plan something after their bedtime. If you're tired, do it anyway; it will refresh you. And, be sure to thank your hubby for chillin' with you.
- *Your Hubby's Preference*: Current research on men's favorite parts of a woman's body shows that most men prefer breasts; however two other parts men prefer are legs and butt. Do you know what your man's preference is? Find out and purchase some lingerie or garment that shows off the asset your man prefers most!
- *One last suggestion*: Choose one day each week, or one day each month, to paper clip or staple to a calendar one to five dollars on the chosen day when you will give your hubby a

special treat. Ask him to choose or choose treats that don't cost a lot of money. Use your imagination. Then save the money each time and see how much you have at the end of the year. Remember, the more treats you give your hubby the more dollars you save! Do the math!

One final note

Committed relationships require continual doses of attention, intention, and action, in order to progress. The same holds true for being a wife your husband can be smitten with and brag about. But the key is to apply yourself daily to your transformation, your marriage, and your life.

The truths, tips, tools, and other essentials in this book have been very successful to those who have tried them. If you take them to heart and mind, you will see great results and benefits as well!

Congratulations on completing this book! May the ingredients in these pages tickle your funny bone (belly), fill your heart, expand your mind, and bless your marriage with as much passion, fun, and love as they have mine. Now go and enjoy the pleasures of your newly rejuvenated wifedom and enjoy your husband!

Our Love Story

Carl & Mavis McKnight

It all began in 1972 at Bret Harte Jr. High, in Los Angeles, Ca. We met but did not connect. In 1973, we were both bussed to Robert Fulton Jr. High, where we did connect. That same semester Carl got kicked out of school and our friendship abruptly ended. He says he knew even then that I was the one for him. In 1976 we re-connected right after High School and dated for one whole week! Then we lost touch with each other and married other people. Then in 1999, after 24 years in a previous marriage, Carl started looking for me. Each time he saw a family member, he would ask, "How is Mavis, what is she doing, is she married or single?" He would always end his inquiry with, "I was supposed to marry her."

Then in June of 2005 my sister gave me an ad from the Los Angeles Sentinel, with his picture in it. He was a real estate loan officer and we were looking for a building and a "hook up". The ad sat in my wallet for 2 months before I called him. When I finally called I thought it was to play games with him. He told me he was a Pastor, invited me to his church anniversary banquet, I made excuses, he countered every excuse, and when the conversation was over I hung up the phone and said, "Have a nice life. I'll never call you again! But God had other plans. No sooner than the thought came in my mind another thought on its heels declared, "That's who you're going to marry." I was flabbergasted! Almost simultaneously, a vision of something white passed through my mind's eye, which turned out to be out wedding and reception set-up!

I made it to the banquet and we decided to go out three weeks later. One date turned into two dates, then three dates. And on the 4th date he popped the question and my answer was yes! His romantic self, invited my father to dinner, asked him for my hand in marriage, and he gave his blessing. Then on April 1, 2006 we stepped into the beginning of our beautiful lives together. Eleven years later, we are happily married, in love, and in the place God intended us to be. This was destiny. God put us together to bring His vision of marriage to life!

Marriage Characteristics

On multiple occasions this question was posed to us: *"If you could teach couples only one thing about how to have a successful relationship, what would it be?"*

Without hesitation we said, *"Couples should look at what characterizes their relationship. We understand every marriage is unique, but there are common things you can strive toward to create and maintain a fulfilling and satisfying relationship."*

We thought it might be helpful to list many of the things that characterize our relationship, as well as the things we do and don't do that add to our relationship success. These lists are by no means complete but simply a majority of what represents our marriage.

What characterizes our relationship: Love; maturity; respect; playfulness; flirting; fun; excitement; fantastic sex; willingness; giving; romance; care and concern; humor; happiness; personal growth; encouragement; support; affirmations; honesty; friendship; good communication; acceptance; patience; courteousness; thoughtfulness; connectedness, bondedness; flow; words and deeds of affection; understanding; and recognition of our individual gifts.

What we do: Laugh; travel; talk; hug; hold hands; kiss; go on dates; nurture one another; check-in with each other; hold one another accountable; constructively correct one another; allow one another freedom to utilize what speaks to us in the area of personal growth and development; and cherish our relationship with God.

What we don't do: Fight; argue; curse; yell; scream; put each other down; cruelly criticize or judge; or use physical abuse. When we find ourselves attempting to control each other, getting irritated, short-tempered, or snappy, we pull back, regroup, apologize if necessary, and remember the love we have for each other.

If this list intimidates you or seems unrealistic, remember that progress takes time. This didn't happen overnight for us, but we both had the desire and understanding to be equally committed to nurturing our marriage. Our suggestion: Try it and you will love it!

Now see if you can list what characterizes your relationship and what positive changes you can add. Have an amazing time with it!

Oh and by the way, the third time was a charm!

Acknowledgements

I must first thank my heavenly Father for giving me this opportunity. I am truly grateful. I know with certainty that He clearly spoke to me about creating a ministry to Christian wives. I tried several times to expand it to all women, but He put a conviction on me each time that it was for Christian wives. He let me know that I was to work with this group first, because they need to stay married, pray and work things out, and protect the children. So, I must obey.

Lorraine Pintus, my mentor and writing coach, who has a heart of gold. Thank you for your sincerity, your sistah love, your hospitality, and the straight-forward and direct way you dealt with me when I lost my motivation and wanted to quit. I am truly grateful for you. You are a pioneer on Intimacy and Christian Marriage, and you encouraged me to write this book. I couldn't have done it without you!

My garden of heros, my children Shaundrea, Jamaal, and Malik, without whom my life would not be the same, and I would not be as inspired to dream. Thank you for your continued encouragement and belief in me. May all your dreams and desires be as magnificent in the outside world as they are within you.

Elisha Holloway for my initial cover designs and your unwavering support. Your willingness to work with me until we, "got it right" speaks volumes about you. Your heart and your input are priceless. Thank you!

Melanie Grace for the final cover design, your gift and talent to make it all happen, and your support and friendship. I am forever grateful!

Jan Edwards, my editor. You did an amazing job! Thank you for your suggestions, ideas, and expertise. You understood my vision and kept me on track. You put in extra time when you didn't have to and I appreciate you for that. You are gifted and magnificent at what you do. Thank you so much for everything.

My Inner Circle and Book Reviewers, Valerie Queen, Shaundrea Menefield, Michele Thomas, Cynthia Lawrence, Deb Shephard, Maurissa Mitchem, Delicia Tyson, and Jeannetta Diamond. You are all amazing and so supportive. Thank you for your input, and continued encouragement.

Cheryl Price, my sister and weekly Coffee Bean buddy, who listened to me talk about it for months. Thank you for your creativity, ideas, fire, advice, insight, support, and referrals. You are one of a kind!

My church family, the members of Life Enrichment Worldwide Ministries. Thank you for letting me be me and for supporting this project.

And what would all of this be without the support of my amazing husband Carl McKnight, a man God saw fit to bless me with. I love you to the moon and back. You touch something deep inside of me and make me feel so special. You inspire me to do my best and be my very best self.

What a caring, supportive, loving, thoughtful, romantic man you are, and so superbly interested in my happiness; and so talented too. Thank you for everything, including my professional headshot that graces the back cover.

I am truly blessed, and my wish and hope is that every woman has the opportunity to be as blessed in matrimony as I am.

Source References

2005 United States National Social Life, Health, and Aging Project. Retrieved from http://www.norc.org/Research/Projects/Pages/national-social-life-health-and-aging-project.aspx

Brock, F. How to get to know yourself in 5 foolproof steps. [Blog post]. Retrieved from http://www.prolificliving.com/the-greatest-discovery-of-all-getting-to-know-yourself/

Dean, B. (2012, June 30). Are you marriage material? 8 Signs You May Not Make a Good Wife. [Blog post]. Retrieved from http://madamenoire.com/192697/are-you-marriage-material-7-signs-you-may-not-make-a-good-wife/

Dictionaryreference.com. Retrieved from www.dictionaryreference.com.

Dillow, Linda and Pintus, Lorraine. *Intimate Issues: 21 Questions Christian Women ask about Sex.* Colorado Springs: Waterbrook Press, 1999

Domino, Connie. *The Law of Forgiveness.* New York: Berkley Books, 2009

Dunn, Jancee. 2017. The Science of Marriage. Time Magazine, pg. 66.

Eggerichs, Emerson. *Love and Respect: Motivating your Man God's Way.* 2002

Estroff, H. 2009, July. Jealousy: The Love Destroyer. *Psychology Today*

Field, David. *Marriage Personalities.* Oregon: Harvest House,1986

Gottman, John and Nan, Silver. *Why Marriages Succeed or Fail: And How You Can Make Yours Last.* New York: Simon & Schuster Publishers, 1994

Hyatt, M. (2011, May 16). 3 Reasons Why You Must Guard Your Heart. [Blog post]. Retrieved from https://michaelhyatt.com/three-reasons-why-you-must-guard-your-heart.html

Kimbro, Dennis and Hill, Napolean. *Think and Grow Rich: A Black Choice.* New York: Ballantine Books, 2011

Larimar, Walt and Barb. *His Brain, Her Brain: How Divinely Designed Differences Can Strengthen Your Marriage.* Michigan: Zondervan, 2008

Omarian, Stormie. *The Power of a Praying Woman.* Oregon: Harvest House Publishers, 2002

Smith, Aja. Married Women Rock. [Blog post] Retrieved from http://www.marriedwomenrock.com/category/my-marriage-blog/

The Bible, New International Readers Version (NIRV) and New King James Version (NKJV)

Williamson, Marianne. *A Return to Love: Reflections on the Principles of "A Course in Miracles".* California: Hayhouse, 1996

Recommended Resources

BOOKS

The Meaning of Marriage, Timothy Keller with Kathy Keller

And They Were Not Ashamed, Dr. Laura Brotherson

The Five Love Languages, Gary Chapman

Feel the Fear and do it Anyway, Dr. Susan Jeffers

Passion Principles, Shannon Etheridge

To learn more about Sex Solutions in marriage, visit the website at www.askcoachmavis.com.

Feel free to contact Mavis McKnight or send comments or questions to askmavis@mavismcknight.com

A referral to www.askcoachmavis.com is most appreciated.

Schedule Mavis to Speak

To schedule Mavis to speak at your organization or women's group, send requests to: askmavis@mavismcknight.com

www.ingramcontent.com/pod-product-compliance
Lightning Source LLC
Chambersburg PA
CBHW051102160426
43193CB00010B/1282